La Caja China Cooking

The Secret to Perfect Roasting

Perry P. Perkins

Elk Mountain Books, Wilsonville, Oregon

La Caja China Cooking

Perry P. Perkins

Published by:

Elk Mountain Books
PO Box 21
Wilsonville, Oregon 97070
info@elkmountianbooks.com

ISBN Print Edition: 1451598017
EAN-13: 9781451598018

Elk Mountain Books titles are available for special promotions and premiums. For details contact: **perry@perryperkinsbooks.com**

Table of Contents

"Cooking is like love.
It should be entered into with wild
abandon…or not at all."

~ Harriet van Horne

Acknowledgments

Every book is a collaboration, and a cookbook more than most.

First and foremost, this book is dedicated to my dad:

Frank Leon Perkins

A master chef, a wonderful father, and an all-around fun guy.

To my fellow foodies at Burnin' Love BBQ:

Christopher Renner and Terry D. Ramsey.

Thanks for helping me stay ever hungry.

To the man behind the magic box:

Roberto Guerra

Thank you for following your own obsession, and blessing
us with La Caja China.

And, as always…to the sweetest dish in my life:

Victoria Kay Perkins

You are patient with my obsessions, first to praise,
and faithful to always try a bite. I love you.

-Perry

Foreword

By Roberto Guerra

Being born in Cuba and raised in Miami by a large family that loves good food; I developed a passion for cooking at a young age. I love fire, which is why I love to barbecue, especially when it involves whole pigs.

My favorite event of the year is our Christmas Eve dinner, when the whole family gets together and roasts a pig, and everyone brings all those great Cuban side dishes like Yuca con Mojo, Congri, and all those great desserts like Bunuelos, Flan (my favorite), and arroz con leche.

Christmas Eve is about more than the food. You get to play dominoes and Mentirosa and just spend time talking to all of your family members.

For many years, I was the person in charge of cooking the pig for Christmas. I loved to do it, but it was, admittedly, getting to be a burden. At the time, we lived in a house with a tiny backyard, and we hardly had any space to cook. What I hated the most was all the preparation required to build a pit and roast the pig; from setting the concrete blocks to preparing the racks that held the pig was always a mission. To this day I don't know where those racks would go every year, but I was never able to find them when I needed them!

I still remember the date, December 23 1985, when my father came to me as I was marinating the pig I was going to roast the next day.

"You know," he said to me, "I have seen a box in Cuba that can cook a pig in half the time and will crispy the skin, guaranteed."

"Oh, really?" I replied, "have you been drinking?

Come on, half the time and a crispy skin? No way!

Then he told me the best part, the part that really freaked me out, "…and the charcoal goes on the top!"

That's it, I said to myself, *my father is going nuts!*

Still, I know my father, and if he told me he had seen such a contraption, then I knew it was true. There and then, we made the decision to build a prototype for testing. Honestly, I was very skeptical about the system. I just wasn't sure it would work. In fact, I was so unsure that I purposely did not bring up the subject the next day, to anyone at the party. By January we had the prototype done, and started cooking right away, trying to get the timing right, and for this we have spent a lot of hours burning charcoal!

Our initial market was the sizable Cuban-American population in the Miami area but has since grown to include barbecue and roasting enthusiasts around the country. Of all the roasting boxes sold last year via the Internet and by telephone, more than 90 percent went to buyers outside the area.

The box has also become the toast of many food writers and celebrity chefs. One feature about the box, in The New York Times, helped triple sales and increase traffic to our website *tenfold*.

In 2009, I have the honor and privilege to "throw down" with celebrity Chef, Bobby Flay, cooking one of my favorite Cuban dishes with La Caja China.

I'm happy to say we won.

Shortly after that I received a call from the far side of the country. A new customer name Perry Perkins, in Oregon, had purchased a Model #2 and had some questions about roasting his first whole pig.

Little did I know that this guy would soon become nearly as obsessed with La Caja China, as I was…and he's not even Cuban! Perry, a professional writer and novelist, began writing and posting recipe articles, using La Caja China to roast some of his own favorite dishes; Texas and Carolina style BBQ - on a *Chinese* box – that he'd ordered from *Miami!*

Those articles, and later the content of his barbeque and grilling blog, which also focused on La Caja China, eventually became the cookbook you're holding right now.

Thank you Perry, for your time, enthusiasm, and dedication to La Caja China. You keep coming up with these amazing recipes…

…and we'll keep making amazing boxes for you to cook them in!

Roberto Guerra, August 2010

Author's Note

La Caja China, for all the pig-related press, is one of the most versatile pieces of equipment I've used in a lifetime of cooking and barbecue.

I can prepare everything from holiday dinners like St. Patrick's Day corned beef and Thanksgiving turkey; ethnic delights like Malaysian Satays and Italian porchetta sandwiches, to Kalua pig and Moroccan lamb. I can grill steaks, braise chickens, and roast prime-rib that rivals any restaurant, and do it all in my own backyard!

And, of course, I can roast melt-in-your-mouth whole pigs that send my guests into fits of gastronomical joy.

Even more importantly, I can prepare these dishes for crowds that would normally require a smoke house, a four-foot deep pit dug in my yard, multiple gas grills, and several full-size ovens. Not only that, but I can do it anywhere, anytime!

La Caja China isn't just about great barbecue and roasting, it's about friends and family, it's about creating memories, and... let's be honest... it's about being "that guy" (or gal) who can make the dinner, holiday, or party, a memorable event.

I bought my first La Caja China to satisfy my obsession with barbecue toys (just ask my long-suffering wife, who has lived with the dozens of grills, barbecues, and cooking gadgets that fill our kitchen, patio, and garage!) I soon found that La Caja China replaced most of my beloved cooking styles in a single, simple, cooking box...and it's on wheels!

If you're looking for a means to roast, grill, bake, braise, smoke, or barbecue...look no further that La Caja China. Cook for a crowd on Model 1, 2 or the awesome new "Semi Pro" model, or create perfect dinners for you own family on Model #3.

If you find something that you can't cook on La Caja China, please send me at email at perry@burninlovebbq.com, or drop by www.burninloveblog.com...and I'll find a way.

I look forward to the challenge!

xi

A note about Roberto Guerra...

One of the biggest reasons I have fallen in love with La Caja China, is because of its creator, Roberto Guerra.

Seldom (if ever) can you purchase something from a major corporation and have your emails and phone calls answered within a day by the company's owner...not in a form letter, but as a personal response to your questions *(try that with your new laptop!)*

In response to my first question about roasting a whole pig, I was surprised (and delighted) to get a phone call that started with, *"Perry, this is Roberto Guerra from La Caja China..."*

In Roberto, I've found a friend who loves what he does, is a master at it, and has a heart to share that love with his customers.

Thank you, Mi Amigo Roberto, for your amazing products, your love of food, family, and fellowship, and your integrity to be "the man behind the box."

-Perry

*"Let the stoics say what they please,
we do not eat for the good of living,
but because the meat is savory
and the appetite is keen."*
- Ralph Waldo Emerson

IN THE BOX

Pierna Criolla a Lo Caja China - 4

Gracie's Luau Pork - 6

Cochinita Pibil - 8

Pulled Porchetta Sandwiches- 10

Carolina Pork Ribs - 12

Suckling Pig - 13

Bourbon Pork Tenderloin - 15

Memphis Whole Pickin' Pig - 16

Dill Lemon Salmon - 19

Polynesian Glazed Salmon - 20

Fire Island Whole Snapper - 21

Whole Stuffed Salmon - 22

Southern Roast Turkey - 23

Cuban Roast Turkey - 25

Caja China Beer Can Chicken - 27

Flattened Mojo Chicken - 29

Peking Duck ala La Cajita China - 31

Chris Renner's True Texas Brisket - 35

New England Corned Beef Dinner - 38

Salt & Pepper Tenderloin - 40

Smokey Beef Ribs - 42

Mexican Barbacoa - 43

Bacon Weave Smoked Meatloaf with Cheddar - 45

Salt Crusted Prime Rib - 46

Doug's Mock Tri-Tip - 48

Castilian Roast Leg of Lamb - 50

Easter Leg of Lamb - 51

Moroccan Whole Roast Lamb - 53

Whole Roasted Goat with Citrus Butter - 55

Hunter's Bear Roast - 58

Pulled, Chopped, or Sliced?

At a Pig Pickin', the barbecue is likely going to be pulled from the bone and served in chunks. This "pulled pork" barbecue is mighty hard to beat. Add a finishing sauce if you like.

The barbecue served in a restaurant is usually chopped, and addition of finishing sauce during chopping is common.

If you decide to go the chopped route, be sure to remember that chopped and pureed ain't the same! Properly cooked barbecue is very tender and slicing is a tricky business when it is warm. Allow the barbecue to cool somewhat for consistent success.

Plunk it between a soft bun of white bread or eat it plain.

Always cook pork shoulders with the fat-cap up, and marinate, wrapped in plastic wrap, 12-24 hours.

Be sure to cook pulled pork to an internal temperature of 195d, and let rest 20-30 minutes before chopping.

Pork should be pulled while warm. My preference is to pull the pork after resting, and mix in some extra rub before serving.

To reheat, spritz with apple juice or drippings, cover tightly with foil, and heat in a 200-250°F oven or smoker, stirring occasionally, until warmed to your liking.

Pierna Criolla a Lo Caja China

Recipe by Roberto Guerra

This is the infamous recipe that Roberto used to defeat celebrity grillmaster Bobby Flay in their Miami Florida ThrowDown!

1 - 8 lb. pork shoulder	8 slices bacon
1/2 lb. ham	1 bottle Malta*
1 cup guava shells*	1 cup Mojo*
1 cup prunes	4 Tbs Adobo*
2 cups brown sugar	2 Tbs sea salt

Debone and flatten meat so that it may be rolled.

If the pork shoulder is very fatty, a small amount may be removed.

Score fat well and marinate for a minimum of 12 hours in the Mojo, and Adobo. Line unrolled roast with ham slices, bacon slices, prunes and guava shells. Roll meat carefully to keep the filling inside. Tie firmly with a butcher cord.

Cover with brown sugar and 1/2 bottle of Malta.

Place Pork shoulders, skin down, between the racks and tie using the 4 S-Hooks.

Place Racks inside the box skin side down, attach probe from the wired thermometer and run wire under short aluminum top frame. Cover box with the ash pan and charcoal grid.

Add 16 lbs. of charcoal for Model #1 Box or 18lbs. for Model #2, or Semi Pro Box and light up. Once lit (20-25 minutes) spread the charcoal evenly over the charcoal grid. Cooking time starts right now.

After 1 hour (1st hour) add 9 lbs. of charcoal (note time).

Continue to add 9 lbs. of charcoal every hour until you reach 195 F on the meat thermometer.

Once you reach 195 F, lift the charcoal grid and shake it well to remove the ashes, now place it on top of the long handles. Do not place on the grass or floor - it will damage them.

Remove the ash pan from the box and dispose of the ashes.

Flip the pork shoulders over to crispy the skin. This is easily done using the patented Rack System, just grab the end of the rack, and lift and slide as you pull upward, using the other hand grab the top end of the other rack and slide it down.

Score the skin using a knife, this helps to remove the fat and crisp the skin. Cover the box again with the ash pan and the charcoal grid; do not add more charcoal at this time.

After 30 minutes, take a peek by lifting the charcoal pan by one end only. You will continue doing this every 10 minutes until the skin is crispy to your liking.

IMPORTANT: Do not open the box until you reach the desired temperature.

These ingredients can be found at most Hispanic groceries, or can be purchased at www.lacajachina.com in a handy recipe pack.

Gracie's Luau Pork

While "babymooning" in Hawaii, my wife and I learned the island tradition of throwing a family luau in honor of a child's first birthday. In celebration of our miracle baby, Grace, we hold this traditional feast each year.

4 - bnls pork shoulders (6lb ea)	4 C hot water
1 ½ gal Hawaiian Mojo	2 Tbs seasoned salt
½ C Stubbs liquid smoke	4 Tbs garlic powder
¼ C Adobo Criollo spices	6 Ti or banana leaves

Marinate pork in Hawaiian Mojo (see recipe) overnight.

Remove from marinade, pat dry, and inject each shoulder with 6-8ozs of remaining marinade.

Score pork on all sides, rub with salt, then brush with liquid smoke, and sprinkle with garlic.

Wrap completely in Ti/Banana leaves, tie with string, and wrap in heavy foil

Place racks inside the box skin side down, attach probe from the wired thermometer and run wire under short aluminum top frame.

Cover box with the ash pan and charcoal grid.

Add 16 lbs. of charcoal for Model #1 Box or 18lbs. for Model #2, or Semi Pro Box and light up. Once lit (20-25 minutes) spread the charcoal evenly over the charcoal grid. Cooking time starts right now. After 1 hour (1st hour) add 9 lbs. of charcoal (note time).

Continue to add 9 lbs. of charcoal every hour until you reach 195 F on the meat thermometer.

Once you reach 195 F, lift the charcoal grid shake it well to remove the ashes, now place it on top of the long handles. Do not place on the grass or floor - it will damage them.

IMPORTANT: Do not open the box until you reach the desired temperature.

Remove the ash pan from the box and dispose of the ashes.

Unwrap foil, peel back the banana leaves, and brush with mojo. Flip the pork shoulders over to crispy the skin.

This is easily done using the patented Rack System, just grab the end of the rack, and lift and slide as you pull upward, using the other hand grab the top end of the other rack and slide it down.

Score the skin using a knife, this helps to remove the fat and crisp the skin. Cover the box again with the ash pan and the charcoal grid; do not add more charcoal at this time.

After 30 minutes, take a peek by lifting the charcoal pan by one end only. You will continue doing this every 10 minutes until the skin is crispy to your liking.

Remove shoulders from Caja and allow to rest 30 minutes.

Chop the meat and then mix with a wash of 1/2 cup liquid smoke, 4 cups hot water, 1/4 cup Adobo Criollo spices, and 2 Tbs seasoned salt.

Let that sit about 15 minutes, drain remaining liquid, and serve with Sweet Hawaiian Pork Sauce (see recipe.)

Note: Traditionally this would be served with white or Hawaiian rice (see recipes.) A nice fruit salad in very complimentary as well.

If you really want to go "Big Island" serve this up with some Lomi-Lomi Salmon, Chicken Long Rice, and Pineapple Haupia. There are many wonderful Hawaiian cookbooks available, my favorite is "Sam Choy's Sampler."

Cochinita Pibil

(Yucatecan Pig)

Cochinita pibil is a traditional Mexican slow-roasted pork dish from the Yucatán Península.

Preparation involves marinating the meat in strongly acidic citrus juice, coloring it with annatto seed, and roasting the meat while it is wrapped in banana leaf.

Traditionally, cochinita pibil was buried in a pit with a fire at the bottom to roast it.

The Mayan word "pibil" means "buried."

3 – 8lb pork shoulders	2½ C fresh lime juice
3 – 4oz packages achiote seasoning	4 lb banana leaves
Pickled red onions, for serving	Habanero salsa

Line three disposable turkey roasting pans with 1 package of banana leaves leaving a overhang on all the edges. Set a pork shoulder into the bottom of each.

Prepare the marinade by breaking the achiote bricks into pieces, and dropping them into a jar. Add the lime juice and 1 tablespoon of salt; blend until the mixture is a smooth, thickish, marinade.

Pour the achiote mixture over the pork, spreading it evenly to coat all surfaces (You'll want to wear latex gloves, since achiote will strain your hands red.)

Fold the overhanging banana leaves over the pork, then use the last package of banana leaves to cover the pork completely. Pour about 3 cups of water over the leaves—it will collect in the bottom of the pan and should be about 1 inch deep.

Place the pans in the bottom of the Caja China, attach probe from the wired thermometer and run wire under short aluminum top frame. Cover box with the ash pan and charcoal grid.

Add 16 lbs. of charcoal for Model #1 Box or 18lbs. for Model #2, or Semi Pro box, and light up. Once lit (20-25 minutes) spread the charcoal evenly over the charcoal grid. Cooking time starts right now. After 1 hour (1st hour) add 9 lbs. of charcoal (note time).

Continue to add 9 lbs. of charcoal every hour until you reach 195 F on the meat thermometer.

IMPORTANT: Do not open the box until you reach the desired temperature.

Once you reach 195 F, lift the charcoal grid shake it well to remove the ashes, now place it on top of the long handles. Do not place on the grass or floor - it will damage them. Remove the ash pan from the box and dispose of the ashes.

Flip the pork shoulders over to crispy the skin. This is easily done using our patented Rack System, just grab the end of the Rack lift and slide as you pull upward, using the other hand grab the top end of the other rack and slide it down.

Score the skin using a knife, this helps to remove the fat and crisp the skin. Cover the box again with the ash pan and the charcoal grid; do not add more charcoal at this time. After 30 minutes, take a peak by lifting the charcoal pan by one end only. You will continue doing this every 10 minutes until the skin is crispy to your liking.

Remove the roasting pans (and pork) from the box, and toss the banana leaves. Test the fork-tender meat with an instant thermometer…it should be between 190 and 195 degrees.

Remove the meat, debone, and coarsely shred it into baking pans, and then slide all the meat, covered with foil, into a low oven, until you're ready to serve.

Pour the juices into a pan, and simmer until reduced by half, season with salt if needed.

Serve with meat on a deep platter with warm corn tortillas, black beans, pickled red onions and habanero salsa. (See recipes.)

Pulled Porchetta Sandwiches

Across Italy, porchetta is usually sold by pitchmen with their typically white-painted vans, especially during public displays or holidays. Porchetta was introduced to the USA by Italian immigrants of the early 20th century.

2 (8lb) pork shoulders	6 Tbs Fennel Seeds
24 cloves garlic, peeled	Salt & pepper
12 Tbs fresh rosemary	2 C red wine
32 oz sliced pancetta	24 crusty Italian rolls
4 C caramelized onions	6 C Italian parsley

Debone and flatten meat so that it may be rolled.

Brush pork with liquid smoke (or smoke with hickory in La Caja China first 2 hours.) Allow liquid smoke to dry on pork at room temp, 1 hour.

Place the fennel, garlic, rosemary, salt, pepper, wine, and pancetta in a food processor and pulse until well mixed. Spread ½ the pancetta mixture evenly over the pork, roll back up and tie tightly. Wrap in aluminum foil and place in the refrigerator for 12 hours or up to two days.

Unwrap pork and place in La Caja China racks. Place racks inside the box skin side down, attach probe from the wired thermometer and run wire under short aluminum top frame. Cover box with the ash pan and charcoal grid.

Add 16 lbs. of charcoal for Model #1 Box or 18lbs. for Model #2, or Semi Pro Box and light up. Once lit (20-25 minutes) spread the charcoal evenly over the charcoal grid. Cooking time starts right now. After 1 hour (1st hour) add 9 lbs. of charcoal (note time).

Continue to add 9 lbs. of charcoal every hour until you reach 195 F on the meat thermometer. Once you reach 195 F, lift the charcoal grid shake it well to remove the ashes, now place it on top of the long handles. Do not place on the grass or floor - it will damage them.

IMPORTANT: Do not open the box until you reach the desired temperature.

Remove the ash pan from the box and dispose of the ashes.

Flip the pork shoulders over to crispy the skin. This is easily done using the patented Rack System, just grab the end of the rack, and lift and slide as you pull upward, using the other hand grab the top end of the other rack and slide it down.

Score the skin using a knife, this helps to remove the fat and crisp the skin. Cover the box again with the ash pan and the charcoal grid; do not add more charcoal at this time.

After 30 minutes, take a peak by lifting the charcoal pan by one end only. You will continue doing this every 10 minutes until the skin is crispy to your liking. Remove shoulders from Caja and allow to rest 30 minutes.

Simmer juices until reduced by half. Keep warm.

Heat the rolls. Place ¼ cup of meat on the warm roll and spoon over a little of the pan juices onto the sandwich.

Top meat with caramelized onions, the ¼ cup of fresh chopped parsley.

Carolina Pork Ribs

In North Carolina's early days, pork was most commonly cooked over an open fire and seasoned with an ordinary table condiment of the time, which consisted of vinegar, salt, red and black pepper, and oyster juice.

Salty vinegar with pepper (but no oyster juice) is basically the same sauce used on most North Carolina barbecue today. The western part of the state usually adds tomato paste of ketchup, as below, for a thicker sauce.

6 racks of pork spareribs   1 ½ C of "Burnin' Love" Rub
1 Qt Carolina Basting Sauce   1 Qt Carolina BBQ Sauce

Prepare ribs by removing the membrane from the underside. Trim off any loose fat or meat. Season ribs with rub, wrap in plastic wrap and let sit in refrigerator overnight.

Allow ribs to warm 1 hour. Place ribs on top of the rack, bone side up. Attach the top rack using the 4 S-Hooks. Place the rack inside the box (still bone side up.) Cover box with the ash pan and charcoal grid.

Add 16 lbs. of charcoal for model #1, or 20 lbs. for model #2, or Semi Pro, and light up. Once lit, (20-25 minutes) spread the charcoal evenly over the charcoal grid. Cooking time starts right now.

After 1 hour open the box by removing both the ash pan and grid together, and place it on top of the long handles. Now flip the ribs bone side down, and brush liberally with a mop, or a non-sugary sauce (or it will burn.)

Replace the ash pan and charcoal grid and add another 10 lbs of charcoal. Cook for an extra 30-45 minutes until done (internal temp 145 degrees F.), peeking in at 10 minute intervals.

If you want to sauce the ribs, do so 5 minutes before they're done and watch carefully.

Suckling Pig

A suckling pig is a piglet fed on its mother's milk and slaughtered between the ages of two and six weeks.

Suckling pig is traditionally cooked whole, often roasted, in various cuisines. It is usually prepared as a treat for special occasions and gatherings.

2 - 12lb suckling pigs	1 lb butter
4 Tbs salt	2 Tbs onion powder
2 Tbsp. garlic powder	4 tsp fresh rosemary
2 tsp ground sage	2 tsp black pepper
2 bunches green onions	4 apples, quartered

A day before cooking, salt and pepper your piglets liberally (we used around 6 tablespoons of salt), both inside and out, and place them uncovered on a wire rack, over a tray, and into your fridge. You want them to be cool and dry.

Melt butter and add all seasonings except green onions. Sauté for 2 minutes then allow to cool. Rub the cavities with the butter mixture and insert the apples and onions.

Place small sticks/blocks in the mouths and, after cooking, replace with a suitable fruit. Cover the ears, snouts and tails with foil to keep it from burning.

Rub a healthy amount of olive oil all over the piglets backs and sprinkle a little more sea salt over them.

Lightly oil La Caja China rack place your piglets on it, belly up, with their legs close to but on the side of the bodies.

Add 16 lbs. of charcoal for Model #1 Box or 18lbs. for Model #2, or Semi Pro Box, and light up. Once lit (20-25 minutes) spread the charcoal evenly over the charcoal grid. Cooking time starts right now.

After 1 hour (1st hour) add 9 lbs. of charcoal (note time).

Continue to add 9 lbs. of charcoal every hour until you reach 195 F on the meat thermometer. Once you reach 195 F, lift the charcoal grid shake it well to remove the ashes, now place it on top of the long handles. Do not place on the grass or floor it will damage them.

Remove the ash pan from the box and dispose of the ashes.

Flip the pigs over to crispy the skin. This is easily done using our patented Rack System, just grab the end of the Rack lift and slide as you pull upward, using the other hand grab the top end of the other rack and slide it down. Score the skin using a knife, this helps to remove the fat and crisp the skin. Cover the box again with the ash pan and the charcoal grid; do not add more charcoal at this time.

After 30 minutes, take a peak by lifting the charcoal pan by one end only. You will continue doing this every 10 minutes until the skin is crispy to your liking. Remove suckings from Caja and allow to rest 30 minutes.

> *We're looking for an "in-the-box" temperature from 250 to 350 F. at around 25 minutes per lb. A suckling pig will likely take ½ the time of a pork shoulder. Make sure to use a digital probe to keep track. The pig is done when the temperature in the thickest part of the ham registers 160 degrees.*

Bourbon Pork Tenderloin

The tenderloin refers to the Psoas major muscle along the central spine portion, which hangs between the shoulder blade and hip socket. This is the tenderest part of the animal, because these muscles are not used for locomotion.

The pork tenderloin is usually sold pre-packaged in larger grocery stores. They are often available both plain and flavored with a marinade. Personally, I tend to be distrustful of anyone's marinade but my own!

2 C white sugar	½ C Jim Beam® Bourbon
2 C water	2 tsp vanilla extract
3 to 4 lbs pork tenderloin	2 tsp black pepper
2 tsp garlic powder	2 Tbs salt

In medium bowl, combine sugar, Jim Beam® Bourbon, water, salt and vanilla. Mix well. Place tenderloins in a large zip bag and pour ½ of marinade over the top. Refrigerate 24 hours.

Season tenderloins with garlic and pepper.

Place in disposable baking dish. Spoon half of sugar mixture over tenderloins, and tent loosely with foil. Place pan(s) in La Caja China.

Add 16 lbs. of charcoal for model #1, or 20 lbs. for model #2, or Semi Pro Box, and light up. Once lit, (20-25 minutes) spread the charcoal evenly over the charcoal grid.

Roast for 20 - 30 minutes. Remove foil and spoon remaining sugar mixture over the tenderloins. Roast 5 more minutes or until pork is golden brown. Cut into 1/4-inch slices and serve with sauce from the pan.

If you're using La Caja China #3, follow the same recipe, but only use 5-8 lbs of coals.

Memphis Whole Pickin' Pig

The first time I cooked a whole pig in my Caja China, my digital thermometer died about fifteen minutes into the process. The good news...I followed the directions printed on the box to a tee, along with the "pig roast worksheet" and the piggie came out perfect!

The only other trouble I ran into was finding out that none of my coolers were big enough to hold the pig, much less the twenty pounds of ice.

Always warn your wife, in advance, that she's going to find a large dead animal in her bathtub...

40-45lb pig, cleaned and butterflied	13oz of table salt
3 C "Burnin' Love BBQ" Rub	½ gallon of water
Memphis Pig Pickin' Baste	Mesquite liquid smoke
Memphis-Style Barbecue Sauce	

Mix up the baste and let it sit at room temperature for 60 minutes or longer. Set aside 4 cups of baste for later use. Mix a brine of ½ gallon of water, and 13oz of table salt. Then Mix 1 part baste with 3 parts brine.

Inject this combination into the pig every 2-3 inches.

Rinse the pig, inside and out, pat dry. Brush the pig down with baste and then rub all over with the seasoning and some fine sea salt. Put pig back in cooler for 24-36 hours (drain the water, and add ice as needed.)

Keep your crushed ice in the bags, instead of just dumping it in your cooler. This will help keep the pig from soaking in a big vat of water. Place a row of bags under, and another over the top.

The day you plan to cook, remove the pig from the cooler and let it warm up to room temperature. This is important for even cooking.

Add 1 cup of mesquite liquid smoke to reserved baste and use this to baste pig before lighting the coals, just before turning, and again after turning.

Then sprinkle the whole pig inside and out with fine sea-salt.

If you have La Caja China's electric smoker attachment, leave out the liquid smoke and burn some apple wood for the first two hours or so.

Place pig between the racks and tie using the 4 S-Hooks.

Cover box with the ash pan and charcoal grid. Add 16 lbs. of charcoal for Model #1 Box or 18lbs. for Model #2, or Semi Pro Box, and light up. Once lit (20-25 minutes) spread the charcoal evenly over the charcoal grid.

Cooking time starts right now.

After 1 hour, add 10 lbs. of charcoal. Continue to add 10 lbs. of charcoal every hour until you reach 195 on the meat thermometer.

> **IMPORTANT: Do not open the box until you reach the desired temperature!**

Once you reach 195, (3-3 ½ hours) lift the charcoal grid shake it well to remove the ashes, now place it on top of the long handles.

Remove the ash pan from the box and dispose of the ashes.

Flip the pig over, baste again, and replace the cover to crispy the skin.

Flipping is easily done using La Caja China's patented Rack System, just grab the end of the rack, and lift and slide as you pull upward, using the other hand grab the top end of the other rack and slide it down.

Score the skin using a knife, this helps to remove the fat and crisp the skin. I just cut a shallow X in each of square of the rack. You want to cut through the skin, but not into the meat.

Cover the box again with the ash pan and the charcoal grid; do not add more charcoal at this time.

After 30 minutes, take a peek, if Ms. Piggy isn't quite as gold and crispy as you wanted, close the lid of another ten. You will continue doing this every 10 minutes until the skin is crispy to your liking.

Once the pig is to your liking, set the lid back on at an angle, so the pig stays warm but isn't cooking, and let it rest for 30-60 minutes…it will still be too hot to touch bare-handed.

For easier carving, lay the whole pig, ribs up (on it's back), and use a boning knife to remove the entire skeleton before slicing or chopping the meat.

Serve with warmed sauce, on the side.

> *Another thing I didn't think of in advance was where I was going to put a piping-hot 45lb pig, once I took it out of the box! Now I have a sheet of plywood, cut to nest on top on the box for storage.*
>
> *I set this up on a couple of saw-horses, or on a picnic table, cover it with a disposable table cloth, and I'm good to go. Just set the pig, rack and all, on the plywood, remove the top half of the rack, and dig in!*

Now, I've cooked a LOT of pork-shoulders over the years, but I've never tasted any pork that compared to this. It was sweet and juicy, and the crispy skin was out of the world!

This was the first (of several) pigs I've done in La Caja China, and it was *so* much easier than I thought it would be. With La Caja China, if you can read the instructions on the side of the box, you too can roast a delicious whole pig!

To make a traditional Cuban roasted pig, follow this same recipe, but substitute Mojo for the Memphis Pig Pickin' Baste, and rub the pig with Adobo Criollo (Cuban style dry rub) instead of the bbq rub.

Be sure to strain the portion of the mojo you intent to inject.

> *I strongly recommend using Kingsford brand charcoal. All of the recipes on La Caja China's website, as well as in this book, are based on Kingsford. Different brands burn at different temperatures and speeds. Just FYI.*

Dill Lemon Salmon

Described and enthusiastically eaten by the Lewis and Clark Expedition, the Chinook salmon is spiritually and culturally prized among certain Native American tribes. Many celebrate the first spring Chinook caught each year with "First Salmon" ceremonies.

This heavy, flavorful fish is named for the Chinook Indians - master traders and fishermen who are now almost gone from the face of the earth, but once enjoyed a peaceful existence along the Columbia River and Northwest Coast.

2 - 6lb Chinook salmon fillets	Salt to taste
1 C butter, melted	1 C lemon juice
4 Tbs dried dill weed	1 Tbs garlic salt
Black pepper to taste	4 C plain yogurt

Line the bottom of La Caja China with foil.

Place salmon in a baking dish. Mix the butter and 1/2 lemon juice in a small bowl, and drizzle over the salmon. Season with salt & pepper.

Combine yogurt, dill, garlic powder, sea salt, and pepper. Spread sauce evenly over salmon.

> *For this recipe you'll need to "pre-heat" the coals, so the salmon will cook quickly, and not dry out.*

Add 16 lbs. of charcoal for Model #1 Box or 18 lbs. for Model #2 or Semi Pro Box and light it up. Once lit (20-25 minutes) spread the charcoal evenly over the charcoal grid.

Move charcoal grid and ash pan to handles and place fillets on the bottom Caja China rack (you won't need the top rack) and tent with foil. Re-cover box with the ash pan and charcoal grid.

Roast 15 minutes, remove foil, and replace lid. Roast an additional 5 minutes or until salmon is easily flaked with a fork.

Plate and spoon extra sauce over.

Polynesian Glazed Salmon

A succulent and tantalizing salmon dish made with garlic, horseradish and pure maple syrup. Be warned, the aroma the escapes your Caja China might cause your guests to swoon.

4 whole salmon fillets
3/4 C pure maple syrup
1 ½ Tbs grated fresh ginger
6 cloves garlic, minced
2 ¼ tsp prepared horseradish

2 sprigs fresh dill
¼ tsp salt
1 C water
½ tsp salt

Combine syrup, water, ginger, 4 cloves of garlic, horseradish and ½ tsp salt in a small saucepan. Bring to a boil; reduce heat to simmer.

Cook until reduced by half, about 15 minutes, and allow to cool.

Glaze will keep refrigerated for several days.

Place salmon fillets in shallow pan. Rub gently with 2 cloves minced garlic, dill and 1/4 teaspoon Salt. Then baste with glaze.

Add 16 lbs. of charcoal for Model #1 Box or 18 lbs. for Model #2 or Semi Pro Box and light it up. Once lit (20-25 minutes) spread the charcoal evenly over the charcoal grid.

Move charcoal grid and ash pan to handles and place fillets on the bottom Caja China rack (you won't need the top rack) and tent with foil.

Re-cover box with the ash pan and charcoal grid.

Roast 15 minutes, remove foil, baste, and replace lid. Roast an additional 5 minutes or until salmon is easily flaked with a fork.

Baste again before serving.

Fire Island Whole Snapper

Bahamians like their food fiery, and this recipe is no exception. Simple to prepare and even simpler to cook in La Caja China, it would be equally delicious with mahi-mahi, bluefish, or striped bass.

If your taste buds are a bit more tender, replace habanero with a milder pepper.

3 whole snapper, 4-5 lbs each	salt and pepper
9 habanero peppers	6 Tbs olive oil
6 large limes	6 large limes, juiced
3 pieces fresh ginger	6 cloves garlic

Rinse fish inside and out. Leave head and tail, but trim away the fins. Blot dry. Slash each fish, to the bone, 3-4 times per side.

Thinly slice peppers (removing seeds), limes, ginger, and garlic, separately.

Rub fish with slices of pepper and lime, sprinkle insides with salt and pepper, then insert a slice of lime, pepper, ginger, and garlic into each slash. Place any remaining in the body cavity of each fish.

Put fish on a platter and pour the lime juice over, sprinkle outsides with salt and pepper. Cover fish with foil and place in refrigerator 30 minutes, while you prep La Caja China.

Add 14 lbs. of charcoal for Model #1 Box or 16 lbs. for Model #2 or Semi Pro Box and light it up. Once lit (20-25 minutes) spread the charcoal evenly over the charcoal grid.

Move charcoal grid and ash pan to handles and place fillets on the bottom Caja China rack (you won't need the top rack) and tent with foil. Re-cover box with the ash pan and charcoal grid.

Roast 40-45 minutes, remove foil, and replace lid. Roast an additional 5 minutes or until snapper is easily flaked with a fork.

Wear gloves when handling these peppers, and be careful not to touch your eyes, face, or any exposed skin.

Whole Stuffed Salmon

2 whole salmon*
4 large onions, diced
8 Tbs parsley, chopped
4 tsp ground oregano
1 tsp black pepper
24 thin slices of lemon

12 slices bacon, diced
12 cloves garlic, minced
½ lb fresh sage, chopped
2 tsp fennel seed
1 tsp sea salt
Olive oil for brushing

*Salmon should be about 8 pounds each, boned for stuffing and scaled

In a skillet, cook diced bacon over low heat until lightly browned, about 2 to 3 minutes. Add onion and garlic; sauté 4 minutes. Remove from heat. Stir in remaining stuffing ingredients. Chill completely.

Lay salmon on work surface, butterflied; season flesh with sea salt and pepper. Lay 3 lemon slices on each side of each salmon.

Spread chilled stuffing on one side and fold other side of salmon over the mixture.

Tie salmon with butcher's twine or use metal skewers to hold Salmon closed. Cover tail with foil.

Brush salmon with Olive Oil.

Add 16 lbs. of charcoal for Model #1 Box or 18 lbs. for Model #2 or Semi Pro Box and light it up. Once lit (20-25 minutes) spread the charcoal evenly over the charcoal grid.

Move charcoal grid and ash pan to handles and place fillets on the bottom Caja China rack (you won't need the top rack) and tent with foil.

Re-cover box with the ash pan and charcoal grid.

Roast 15 minutes, remove foil, and replace lid. Roast an additional 5 minutes or until salmon is easily flaked with a fork.

Southern Roast Turkey

Adapted from my father's, Chef Frank L. Perkins, recipe.

3 12-14lb turkeys, frozen
Smoked paprika
1 ½ C salad oil
9 C white sugar

Salt and pepper to taste
3 C melted butter
9 C fine sea salt

Start with 3 - 5 gallon buckets. Boil 12 cups of water with 9 cups of fine sea salt, and 9 cups white sugar. Allow to cool. Pour 4 cups of seasoned water into each bucket.

Put your frozen turkey in the bucket, and fill with water until you have totally submersed your turkeys, put a weight on each turkey to hold it down. Cover your buckets with towels and leave your turkeys like that over night.

Take the turkeys out of the water the next morning, rinse them clean, and pat dry. Combine oil and melted butter and rub generously on the birds, including inside, and as far under the skin as possible.

Sprinkle turkeys generously with pepper and paprika both inside and outside, and bring to room temp.

Place turkeys on top of the rack, breast up, and attach top rack using the 4 S-Hooks and tent loosely with foil. Attach probe from a wired thermometer and run wire under short top frame.

Cover box with the ash pan and charcoal grid.

Add 16 lbs. of charcoal for model #1 or 20 lbs. for model #2 and light up. Once lit (20-25 minutes) spread the charcoal evenly over the charcoal grid.

Cooking time starts right now.

After 1 hour, add 10 lbs. of charcoal.

After about 1 ½ hours, open the roaster and baste the bird with the stock inside the pan to ensure it has the right amount of tenderness.

After another hour (2.5 hours, total) add 10 lbs. of charcoal.

Do not add any more charcoal; continue cooking the turkeys until you reach the desired temperature reading, on the thermometer of 175 f.

Remove foil and flip the birds. Cover the box again and brown the top of the turkeys 15-20 minutes, to your liking.

Remove birds and pans from La Caja China, reserving the leftover stock for use with your dressing. Drain the excess fat and save for your giblet gravy.

Allow turkey to rest 30 minutes before carving and serving.

Serve with cornbread stuffing and giblet gravy.

Yee-Haw!

Place a shallow, disposable aluminum pan, slightly larger than the turkey itself, beneath the rack under each bird. Not only will this save you some clean-up later, but it will also catch some wonderful drippings that will make the best turkey gravy you've ever had. Thanks, Dad!

Cuban Roast Turkey

3 – 12 to 14 lb turkey	24 tbsp Unsalted butter
Fresh ground pepper	Salt

Marinade

3 garlic heads, peeled	3 C sour orange juice
3 tsp black pepper	4 ½ tsp ground cumin
6 tsp dried oregano	3 Tbs Salt

The day before, remove giblets and any lumps of fat from the turkey cavities. Rinse the turkey properly and blot dry.

Season the inside with salt and pepper and loosen the turkey skin from the meat. To do this, begin at the neck and tunnel your fingers, then whole hand, under the skin to separate the skin from the breast meat.

Slide your hand down to loosen the skin over the thighs, drumsticks and back carefully, so as not to tear the skin.

For the marinade, mash the garlic and salt in a mortar to make a fine paste. Add pepper, cumin, oregano and all the lime juice or sour orange juice and puree the ingredients.

Now add 3 Tbs marinade to the main cavity and 1 tbsp to the neck cavity. Put rest of the marinade under the skin and work over a roasting pan to catch any runoff from the marinade.

Keep the bird in a big plastic bag with any excess marinade, and marinate the turkey overnight in the refrigerator, turning several times.

Thinly cut the butter and put half of the slices under the skin. Melt rest of the butter.

Place turkeys on La Caja China racks, breast side down.

Brush the skin of the turkey with some melted butter, and pour rest of the butter and marinade over the turkeys, and tent foil loosely over each. Attach probe from a wired thermometer and run wire under short top frame.

Cover box with the ash pan and charcoal grid.

Add 16 lbs. of charcoal for model #1 or 20 lbs. for model #2 and light up. Once lit (20-25 minutes) spread the charcoal evenly over the charcoal grid.

Cooking time starts right now.

After 1 hour (2nd hour) add 10 lbs. of charcoal.

After about 1 1/2 hours, open the roaster and baste the bird with the stock inside the pan to ensure it has the right amount of tenderness.

After 1 hour (3rd hour) add 10 lbs. of charcoal.

Do not add any more charcoal; continue cooking the Turkey until you reach the desired temperature reading, on the thermometer of 175 f.

Allow turkey to rest, breast down, 30 minutes before carving and serving.

Caja China Beer Can Chicken

Also known as dancing chicken, chicken on a throne, and the ever-classy "beer in the butt chicken," this has become a hugely popular technique for roasting or smoking whole birds. Beer can chicken is moist and flavorful, with a hint of malt and hops, and for simple cooking with amazing results, this is about the best way there is to cook a chicken.

6 cans (12 ounces) beer
3/4 C La Habana Pork Rub
12 tsp mesquite liquid smoke

6 chickens (4 lbs each)
¼ C vegetable oil

Not necessary, but preferred:
3 - Vertical chicken roasters (2 chickens each)

Open the beer and pour half of each can into a large pitcher. Using a church key-style can opener, punch 2 more holes in the top of each can. Set the can of beer aside. Rinse chickens, inside and out, with cold water. Drain and blot dry.

Sprinkle 1 teaspoon of the rub into each body cavity and ½ teaspoon inside the neck cavity of the chicken.

Mix oil and 6 tsp. liquid smoke and brush generously all over the outside of the birds, beneath the skin where possible. Sprinkle the outside with 1 tablespoon of rub and rub well, again, getting a generous amount beneath the skin of the breasts.

Spoon the remaining rub and liquid smoke evenly into the beer cans. Put cans into vertical chicken roasters, open end up.

Hold each chicken upright, with the opening of the body cavity at the bottom, and lower it onto the a can. Pull the chicken legs forward to form a sort of tripod, so the bird stands upright, with the rear leg of the tripod being the beer can. Place loaded roasters into La Caja China, with a drip pan beneath each, and tent each chicken loosely with foil. If you do not have a roster, balance the chickens carefully on the drip pans.

Using one of the center chickens, insert a thermometer probe into the thickest part of a thigh, but not touching the bone. Add 15 lbs. of charcoal for model #1 or 18 lbs. for model #2 or Semi Pro Box, and light up. Once lit (20-25 minutes) spread the charcoal evenly over the charcoal grid. Cooking time starts right now.

Cook to 180F (about 1 hour), remove foil, and roast, if necessary 5-10 more minutes to brown. Remove chickens from vertical roaster, and allow to rest for 5 minutes (careful not to spill the hot beer!) Halve, quarter, or carve the chicken and serve.

IMPORTANT: Do not open the box until you reach the desired temperature.

Serves 12 to 24

I have, on occasion, replaced the beer in this recipe with pop-canned peach nectar. The results are a completely different, but equally wonderful flavor.

And that leftover pitcher of beer? That's to keep the cook cool while slaving over a hot roasting box!

Flattened Mojo Chicken

A flattened, or "spatchcocked" chicken cooks in less time than a regular chicken and can be grilled or roasted without becoming overcooked. Mojo [MOH-hoh] is considered the signature marinade of Cuba, and is used to complement a wide variety of foods such as beef, pork and poultry.

6 - 4lb whole chickens	6 Tbs olive oil
12 C Traditional Cuban Mojo	6 tsp sea salt
6 Tbs Adobo Criollo spice blend	

Rinse chicken with cold water and pat dry. Cut out backbone with kitchen shears.

Turn chicken breast side up and open like a book. Press down firmly on breast to flatten and break rib bones. Loosen skin from body under breast and thighs.

Place each chicken in a gallon-size resealable bag with 2 cups Mojo. Marinate (flat) in refrigerator 24 hours.

Remove chickens from bags and discard mojo. Blot each bird dry, and rub each with 1 Tbs olive oil, and then 1 Tbs Adobo Criollo spice blend.

Place chickens (flattened) breast up on a roasting pan with a rack, and sprinkle with salt.

Add a couple of cups of warm water to each pan, and tent each chicken loosely with foil.

Using one of the center chickens, insert a thermometer probe into the thickest part of a thigh, but not touching the bone.

Add 15 lbs. of charcoal for model #1 or 18 lbs. for model #2 or Semi Pro Box, and light up. Once lit (20-25 minutes) spread the charcoal evenly over the charcoal grid.

Cooking time starts right now.

Cook to 170F (about 1 hour), remove foil, and roast, if necessary 5-10 more minutes to brown.

Remove chickens from La Caja China, and allow to rest for 5 minutes.

Halve, quarter, or carve the chicken and serve with Quick Saffron Basmati Rice.

IMPORTANT: Do not open the box until you reach the desired temperature.

Serves 12 to 24

Both Cuban Mojo and Authentic Cuban Adobo Criollo can be purchased directly from La Caja China at www.lacajachina.com (under "Mojo & Spices.")

Peking Duck ala La Cajita China

Duck has been roasted in China since the Southern and Northern Dynasties. A variation of roast duck was prepared for the Emperor of China in the Yuan Dynasty. The dish, originally named "Shaoyazi," was mentioned in the Complete Recipes for Dishes and Beverages manual in 1330 by Hu Sihui, an inspector of the imperial kitchen.

Beijing's most famous dish, Peking Duck is traditionally served with Mandarin pancakes. I've modified this dish slightly for roasting in La Cajita China.

2 – 5 to 6 pound ducks	12 C water
¼ C powdered ginger	6 scallion, cut into halves
½ C honey	¼ C rice wine vinegar
½ C sherry	Scallions for garnish
6 tablespoons cornstarch	

Clean ducks. Wipe dry and place each duck on a "beer-can chicken" stand. Set in a cool room in front of a fan for 4 hours to dry. (See note.)

Bring a large pot with water to boil, and add ginger, scallion, honey, vinegar, and sherry. Boil 10 minutes, then pour in the dissolved cornstarch, stirring constantly.

Place one duck in boiling water, count to five and remove. Place the second duck in boiling water, count to five and remove. Repeat for 10 minutes.

Place ducks on "beer can" racks again, in front of fan, for 6 hours until thoroughly dry. Turn every 30 minutes.

"Pre-heat" La Cajita China with 10lbs of charcoal. When all coals are covered in white ash, oil the roasting rack (pre-heated) and place ducks, breast side up, on rack.

WARNING – Edges of the box will be *very* hot, be careful not to touch them when placing the ducks inside.

Place the rack in the roasting pan with 2 inches of water in bottom, and close up the box, and add another 5lbs of charcoal.

You goal temperature inside the box is 350 degrees.

Roast 20 minutes.

Turn ducks, add 5lbs of charcoal, and roast 20 minutes more. Turn breast side up again. Roast 5 minutes more, until crispy and browned to your liking.

Remove ducks from La Cajita China and allow to rest 10-15 minutes.

Use sharp knife to debone. Serve meat and skin immediately on a pre-warmed dish.

The duck is eaten hot with hoisin sauce rolled in Mandarin Crepes. Garnish with diced scallion.

Each duck serves 3 to 4

Drying: I set my ducks up on "beer-can chicken" stands (instead of hanging them by the necks — the traditional method), in front of a fan, and turned them every 30 minutes. Worked perfectly!

Brisket Tips

Preparing: If you have a frozen brisket, let it thaw in the refrigerator for 2 days to defrost thoroughly. Two hours before you plan to begin cooking, take the brisket from the refrigerator. Remove the plastic packaging, rinse brisket well with cool water, and pat dry.

DO NOT remove the fat; that will provide moisture and flavor as the brisket cooks.

Reheating: Spritz the meat with apple juice and add 1/8" of the same juice to the bottom of the pan. Cover tightly with foil and heat in a 200-250°F oven until warmed to your liking. Just before serving, brush on a thin layer of your favorite barbecue sauce to give the slices a nice sheen.

If you prefer to keep the cooked brisket whole and unsliced, wrap it in foil and refrigerate. Before reheating, open the foil and add some juice or broth as described above, and close the foil tightly.

Heat in the oven or smoker at 200-250°F until warmed to your liking, then slice and serve.

Resting Time: At a minimum, place the brisket on a rimmed baking pan, cover loosely with foil, and let rest 30 minutes before slicing. 60-90 minutes is better.

Brisket Yield: When you take into account the trimming of the brisket before and after cooking, plus the shrinkage that occurs during cooking, don't be surprised if you end up with a 50% yield of edible meat from a whole, untrimmed brisket.

That means 6 pounds of edible meat from a 12 pound brisket.

Depending on the brisket and the internal temp you cook it to, it may be as low as 40% or as high as 60%.

If you're cooking brisket for a party, figure 4-5 ounces of meat per sandwich or 6 ounces of sliced meat on a plate (8 ounces for hearty eaters). Using a 40% yield, just to be safe, a 12 pound brisket yields 19 4-ounce sandwiches or almost 13 6-ounce plate servings.

Burnt Ends: Traditionally, burnt ends sold in restaurants were the dry edges and leftover bits and pieces of the brisket flat after slicing, mixed with barbecue sauce. These morsels were highly prized for their intense, smoky flavor.

Today, famous barbecue joints like Arthur Bryant's in Kansas City can't meet the demand for burnt ends using leftover bits, so they make a facsimile by cubing fully cooked brisket flats, placing the cubes in a pan and smoking them for a couple of hours, then adding sauce and smoking for a couple more hours.

Another approach for making burnt ends is to separate the point section from the flat section after the flat is done, then return the point to the cooker for smoke for an additional 4-6 hours. Chop the point, mix with barbecue sauce, and enjoy!

True Texas Brisket

Recipe by Christopher Renner

In Texas, barbecue means beef, particularly untrimmed brisket, that's been slow-cooked over coals or wood in above ground smokers

No sauce is used before or during cooking. Pepper and salt are the most common seasonings. A thick tomato-based sauce with a sweet and spicy taste is served on the side of the barbecue meal.

Beans, potato salad and thick toasted white bread called Texas Toast are often added to the meal.

> 4 whole (packer-style) briskets, 12-14lbs each.
> 6 C Renner's Amazing Brisket Rub
> 8 C Sweet Brisket Mop (optional)
> 1 (each) Oak & Pecan smoke bullets

Everything can be ready ahead of time: mix the dry rub and make the basting sauce days ahead of time; have the charcoal and heavy-duty aluminum foil on hand.

Brisket: Buy an untrimmed (sometimes called packer style) brisket available at most grocery stores. It will have a thick cap of fat, and is usually in heavy plastic packaging.

Four 14-pound briskets fits nicely in La Caja China; briskets are available in sizes from about 8 pounds and up. Calculate about 2 servings per pound. Don't underestimate quantity, as you probably won't have much left over!

The night before you plan to begin cooking, rinse the briskets, and pat dry. Place the briskets in large disposable pans and generously apply the dry rub, to all meat surfaces. Refrigerate overnight.

Mix the pellets from one canister of oak and one of pecan, and refill both.

Once hour before cooking, remove the briskets from the cooler and let stand at room temperature until cooking time.

Place the brisket on the meat rack in La Caja China, fat side up, and set disposable catch pans beneath the lower rack to catch the drippings. Cover the box with the ash pan and charcoal grid, and add 16 lbs. of charcoal for Model #1, or 18lbs. for Model #2 and light up. Allow about 20 minutes for coals to burn evenly.

After 20 minutes, spread the coals evenly over the surface of the charcoal pan. Cooking time starts right now.

Start the smoker unit and run the first 3 hours. If you don't have the electric smoker unit, top upper rack with a pan of wood chips (about 2 cups.)

After 1 hour (1st hour) open the box, flip the meat over, connect the wired thermometer probe in the center of the meat, close the box and add 10 lbs. of charcoal.

Continue to add 10 lbs. of charcoal every hour until you reach the desired temperature on the meat thermometer.

IMPORTANT: *DO NOT OPEN THE BOX UNTIL YOU REACH THE DESIRED TEMPERATURE!*

Once you've cooked the briskets to an internal temperature above 190 degrees F, it's time to wrap them.

Remove the briskets from La Caja China, mop with warmed sauce (optional) and wrap each in a double layer of aluminum foil as tight as you can. The internal temperature will continue to climb.

Wrap the foil-wrapped briskets in towels and place the in an empty cooler. Let the briskets sit for 60 to 90 minutes before checking the internal temperature again. Once you reach 190 degrees your briskets are cooked and rested.

Slicing the briskets:

Cut back the fat layer on the top of the brisket to expose the meat. Then, working from the thin end of the brisket, cut long thin slices about the thickness of a pencil, against the grain of the meat, paying attention as the grain direction changes.

If you find that the brisket is a little tough, cut it thinner. If the brisket starts to fall apart, cut the slices thicker. Trim off any large pieces of fat as you go.

I like to place my cutting-board with one end over the edge of the sink and the other end propped up slightly. Place a pan in the bottom of the sink to catch the juices that run out as you go. These can be poured back over the meat after it's carved.

You'll have several cups of meat juices trapped in the pans as well. Save any juices that you don't serve with the meat, it's great in beans and sauces.

Serve immediately with finishing sauce and sliced white bread.

By the way, the big bed of glowing coals is great for grilling some fresh corn on the cob. . Soak the corn (in husks) in cold water to cover for about an hour. Shake off excess moisture and place directly on the coals.

Roast, turning frequently, for 30 - 45 minutes.

Reserve brisket juices, meat trimmings and burnt ends to make Brisket Beans later (see recipe.)

Your briskets will probably come out of the box black and charred, especially is you used a sugar-based rub. Don't panic!.)

The brisket is placed fat-side up for just this reason, to protect the meat. This fat cap will be sliced and tossed later, anyway. 50 pounds of brisket will generously serve 100 people. The meat is very rich and diners who are unfamiliar with it often take more that they can eat. I always serve the brisket myself, at the end of a buffet-line, when I cook for a crowd.

If you'd like to see this recipe, with step-by-step photos, make sure to visit www.burninloveblog.com

---

New England Corned Beef Dinner

In the US and Canada, consumption of corned beef is usually associated with Saint Patrick's Day. Ironically, corned beef isn't native to Ireland, and only became popular in US after Irish immigrants in the east used corned beef instead of pork in their traditional bacon joints and cabbage dish.

The classic New England "boiled" dinner includes corned beef with rutabagas, carrots, onions, potatoes, and cabbage.

4 corned briskets, 4lbs each	4 med cabbage wedges
4 small bay leaves	24 peppercorns
12 rutabagas, cut in chunks	4 lbs carrots, peeled
24 sweet onions, halved	4 C brown mustard
24 medium potatoes, peeled	

To make the mop, bring 1 gallon of water to a simmer with bay leaves, peppercorns, and spice packets (in included) from corned beef. Simmer 10-15 minutes, allow mop to cool until just warm.

Two hours before cooking, remove the corned beef from the refrigerator and let stand at room temperature until cooking time.

Place the corned beef on the rack in La Caja China, fat side up, and set disposable catch pans beneath the lower rack to catch the drippings.

Pour the mop evenly over each corned beef, tent each loosely with foil, and insert a probe thermometer into the thickest part of one beef.

Cover the box with the ash pan and charcoal grid, and add 16 lbs of charcoal for Model #1, or 18lbs for Model #2 and Semi Pro Box, and light up.

Allow about 20 minutes for coals to burn evenly. After 20 minutes, spread the coals evenly over the surface of the charcoal pan.

Cooking time starts right now.

While meat is cooking, divide rutabagas, onions, potatoes, and cabbages evenly between 4 disposable turkey roasting pans, have eight large sheets of foil torn and ready.

Roast briskets until internal temperature reaches 180d, then, working quickly (this is a good time to have a partner) remove the ash pan and grid, lift the full rack out of La Caja China, open, and place one corned beef in each turkey pan, on top of vegetables.

Pour any drippings evenly over the meat (toss the drip pans), and seal each pan with a double layer of heavy foil.

Insert the probe into the thickest part of one beef, and place all 4 pans into La Caja China. Cover the box with the ash pan and charcoal grid, and add 10 lbs of charcoal for Model #1, or 15lbs for Model #2 and Semi Pro Box.

Add 10 lbs of charcoal every hour until you've cooked the corned beef to an internal temperature above 190 degrees F.

IMPORTANT: *Do not open the box until you reach the desired temperature.*

Remove pans from La Caja China. Smear the meat-side of each corned beef with 1 cup of mustard and wrap, fat side down, in a double layer of foil, wrap each of these a towel, and place in a tight cooler for 60-90 minutes.

Combine veggies (and broth) into two turkey pans, cover, and keep (just) warm in oven.

After 90 minutes, allow the meat to rest at room temp, unwrapped, 15-20 minutes, then slice thinly across the grain, disposing of excess fat.

Serve corned beef surrounded with vegetables.

Corned beef dinner serves 30 to 40

Salt & Pepper Beef Tenderloin

The whole beef tenderloin roast is sometimes called a "whole filet," a "filet mignon roast," or a "tenderloin tip roast."

It's a long, tapered muscle located on the inside of the short loin, extending from the 13th rib to the pelvis. As the name suggest, it is one of the most tender cuts of beef you can prepare.

3 whole beef tenderloins	1 C fine sea salt
3/4 C olive oil	6 Tbs black pepper

Buy the tenderloins pre-trimmed, around 5-6 lbs each.

Pre-cut 7-8 pieces of kitchen twine, each about 18" long, for each tenderloin.

Fold the tail under the center section to create an even diameter, and tie up each tenderloin evenly with 8 pieces of twine. Trim any loose ends.

Pat dry with paper towels and sprinkle all sides with 1-1/2 tablespoons of salt.

Wrap in plastic wrap and let sit at room temperature for one hour. This step allows the salt to penetrate the meat and will help it cook more evenly.

Just before cooking, apply a thin coat of olive oil and sprinkle with a good amount of freshly cracked black pepper.

Place tenderloins on bottom roasting rack (no top rack required), in La Caja China and tent loosely with foil.

Insert a probe thermometer into center tenderloin.

Add 16 lbs of charcoal for model #1, or 20 lbs for model #2, or Semi Pro Box, and light up.

Once lit, (20-25 minutes) spread the charcoal evenly over the charcoal grid. Roast until tenderloins reach 120-125°F for rare/medium-rare.

IMPORTANT: Do not open the box until you reach the desired temperature.

If necessary, add 10lbs of charcoal after the first hour until tenderloins reach 120-125°F for rare/medium-rare.

Remove meat from box, place cooking grate directly over hot coals, and sear tenderloin on all sides, approximately 2 minutes per side.

Cover loosely with foil and let rest for 10 minutes before thin slicing across the grain.

You can serve these tenderloin rounds as high-class sliders (for a big crowd) or with your favorite steamed veggie and Ma Geisert's Cheesy Potatoes.

Smokey Beef Ribs

Beef Ribs may not be the pit-master poster child that pork ribs are, but these "dinosaur bones" of beefy goodness make for awesome barbecue, and they're often a great deal at the grocery store, as well.

Like pork ribs, if done wrong they can be tough and stringy, but when done right they're tender, juicy and full of flavor.

Plan on about 3 ribs per person, and you'll have a full and happy crew!

6 full beef rib racks, trimmed	1 C dry rub
3 C rib mop	3 C finishing sauce
2-3 cans of beer	

The night before cooking, rub beef ribs and wrap in plastic. Refrigerate 12-18 hours.

Place disposable pans beneath the lower rack and pour a can of beer (or more) into each. There should be at least an inch of beer in each.

Allow ribs to come to room temp, then lay them across the bottom rack, face down in the box. Tent ribs loosely with foil, and close the box.

Add 16 lbs. of charcoal for model #1 or 20 lbs. for model #2, divided into two piles, and light up. At 30 minutes, spread coals over surface. Cooking time starts now. Start smoke pistol, and smoke with oak wood, for the first 2 ½ hours of cooking time.

At 1 hour (cooking time), lift the lid and quickly mop the ribs, re-tent with foil (add more beer if necessary,) close La Caja China, and add another 10lbs of unlit coals.

After 2 hours (cooking time), – flip ribs "face up", mop again, remove the foil, and close the box to brown the top of the ribs. Check every 15 minutes until the ribs are browned to your liking.

Serve with finishing sauce (warmed) on the side.

You may want to remove the whole lower rack to serve the ribs. While they shouldn't be "falling off the bone," a long rack can still split apart at this phase.

Mexican Barbacoa

The ancient tradition of barbacoa, which is where we get the word "barbecue," runs deep within the culture of Mexico. In the original, Indian pit-cooking process, the meat was seasoned, wrapped in either maguey or banana leaves, then placed on a grill over a cauldron of water that is set over glowing coals in a pit about three feet deep.

The following recipe uses chuck roast for South Texas style barbacoa, and no need to dig a hole when you have La Caja China!

4 - 3 ½ lb bone-in chuck roast
2 Tbs cumin
2 Tbs dried oregano
2 Tbs smoked paprika
1/4 cup mesquite liquid smoke*

1/4 C garlic powder
2 Tbs black pepper
4 Tbs chile powder
2 Tbs fine sea salt

Or use smoke pistol w/ oak pellets

Combine all spices and liquid smoke into a paste (if using smoke pistol, combine spices into a dry rub) and rub into all sides of the roasts. Wrap roasts in plastic wrap and refrigerate 24 hours. Allow roasts to rest 1 hour at room temperature.

Place roast on La Caja China bottom rack and place rack in La Caja China, over shallow drip pans. Insert probe thermometer into thickest part of center roast.

Cover the box with the ash pan and charcoal grid, and add 16 lbs. of charcoal for Model #1, or 18lbs. for Model #2 and light up. Allow about 20 minutes for coals to burn evenly. After 20 minutes, spread the coals evenly over the surface of the charcoal pan.

Cooking time starts right now.

Start the smoker pistol (if you have one) with oak pellets, and run the first hour.

Roast to internal temp of 160 - 170 degrees, then remove roasts, seal each with heavy duty aluminum foil, and return to La Caja China.

> **IMPORTANT:** Do not open the box until you reach the desired temperature.

Add another add 10 lbs. of charcoal, and roast another hour.

Remove the packages from the box, and place it in a large, paper, grocery bags. Fold each bag tightly to seal it and leave it for 45 minutes.

Remove the meat from the roasting pan and shred into small pieces.

Serve with Bubba's Easy Guacamole, your favorite salsa, and hot tortillas.

> *If you're a true chile-head, roast some whole jalapeños over the coals, slice, core (to remove the seeds) and serve on the side.*

Bacon Weave Meatloaf with Blue Cheese

3 lbs ground sirloin
4 scallions finely chopped
3 Tbs bbq sauce
Bread crumbs to bind.

1 lb bacon (to wrap)
1 tsp minced garlic
½ lb blue cheese

Mixed together all of the ingredients, except bacon, and add just enough bread crumbs to bind it together. Weave bacon into a square mat, top with meat mixture and roll into a log, with bacon completely covering the outside. Tuck bacon around ends to cover.

Wrap meatloaf in foil and place in La Cajita China, and insert probe thermometer. Put top tray on roaster and build fire, using 5 pounds of charcoal (1 chimney) in center of charcoal pan. Spread coals after 20 minutes.

Roast to internal temperature of 160d, remove from La Caja China, unwrap, and allow to rest 15 minutes before slicing and serving.

For a crispy exterior, allow the roast to rest 15 minutes, and then place on La Caja China Grill, turning until brown on all sides. This recipe can be double or tripled for a single meal.

Salt Crusted Prime Rib

The traditional preparation for a standing rib roast is to rub the outside of the roast with salt and seasonings and slow-roast with dry heat. In the United States, it is common for barbecue purists to apply smoke to the uncooked rib roast at low heat for 2-3 hours before dry roasting. In the United Kingdom, Yorkshire pudding is frequently served as a side dish with prime rib.

1 ½ C coarsely ground black pepper   1 C kosher salt
2 head of garlic, peeled   1 C fresh rosemary
4 Tbs smoked paprika powder   1 ½ C olive oil
2 - 16-pound prime rib roasts (6 bones)

In a food processor, combine the salt, pepper, garlic cloves, rosemary and paprika, and process until fine. Add the olive oil and pulse to form a paste. Pat the rib roast dry with a paper towel or napkin.

Place the prime rib roasts on a cutting board, bone-side up and rub each with 1 tablespoon of the salt paste.

Pack the salt paste all over the fatty surface of both roasts, pressing to help it adhere. Let the prime ribs stand at room temperature for 2 hours.

Insert meat thermometer so tip is in thickest part of beef, not resting in fat or touching bone.

Place disposable pans beneath the Caja China rack to catch the drippings, tent ribs loosely with foil, and close the box.

Add 16 lbs. of charcoal for model #1 or 20 lbs. for model #2 or Semi-Pro Box, divided into two piles, and light up.

At 30 minutes, spread coals over surface. Cooking time starts now.

At 1 hour (cooking time), lift the lid and quickly baste the roasts, and re-tent with foil. Dump excess ashes, close La Caja China and add another 10lbs of unlit coals.

After 2 hours (cooking time), – baste again, remove the foil, and close the box to brown the top of the roasts.

Cook until rib roasts reach an internal temperature of 120 degrees F. Then remove the foil and brown 10 to 15 minutes longer.

Remove the roasts from La Caja China, cover with aluminum foil, transfer the roasts to a large carving board, and let the meat rest for 30 minutes

Remember, the rib roast will continue to cook as it sets. The temperature will rise from 125 degrees F to 130-135 degree internal temperature (medium rare) at 15 to 20 minutes.

If allowed to rest as long as an hour, the temperature will rise even higher.

Carefully lift the salt crust off the meat and transfer to a bowl. Brush away any excess salt.

To remove the roast in one piece while keeping the rib rack intact, run a long sharp carving knife along the bones, using them as your guide.

Carve the prime rib roast 1-inch thick and serve, passing some of the crumbled salt crust as a condiment.

Doug's Mock Tri-Tip

Recipe by Doug Fairrington

My buddy Doug jokes that he's too cheap for tri tip! Luckily, he's a master griller and has had great results with applying the same cooking methods to cheaper cuts of beef, like chuck. The key with these muscle cuts, he says, lies in taking as long as possible to get them to 145 degrees.

Use an herb/spice butter to help add moisture, and an instant-read thermometer, so you don't have to cut into meet to check for doneness, allowing valuable juices to escape.

2 - 4 lbs chuck roast, cut 2" thick	1 Tbs garlic powder
1 Tbs onion powder	1 Tbs celery salt
1 tsp oregano	Italian dressing

Steak butter

1 lb sweet cream butter	4 Tbs seasoned salt
2 Tbs garlic powder	2 Tbs smoked paprika
1 Tbs coarse black pepper	

Using 10lbs of charcoal, build a two-zone fire on La Cajita China.

Marinade meat overnight in oil and vinegar based Italian dressing, remove from marinade, and blot dry. Mix all spices and rub both sides of roasts, then let stand at room temperature for 1 hour.

Warm butter and add seasoned salt, garlic, paprika, and pepper, blending well. Cool slightly until spreadable.

Place roasts on grill, over the "hot end" of the fire.

If you'd like a little smoke, scatter a small handful of oak chips, or pellets, on the coals as well. Sear both sides, about 5 minutes per side.

Remove the ash pan and grate, and place the roast on the interior rack, over a drip pan.

Smear the top of roasts with 1/2 of the steak-butter, insert a probe thermometer into the thickest part of one roast, and close the box.

Spread the coals out evenly.

Add 5lbs of coals every hour (10 for larger models) until roasts reach an internal temperature of 145d.

IMPORTANT: Do not open the box until you reach the desired temperature.

Remove roasts from La Cajita China, flip, and smear with remaining steak-butter, and allow to rest 15 minutes to before cutting in 1/8 " slices across the grain. Serve.

This recipe is designed for La Caja China Model #3, but could be doubled, or tripled, on the larger boxes, starting with 15lbs of coals instead of 10.

Castilian Roast Leg of Lamb

This is a popular dish around the north of Madrid, especially during the Christmas season.

2 - 9 lb legs of lamb (bone in)	4 tablespoons of olive oil
Freshly ground black pepper	Salt
2 teaspoon fresh thyme	4 cloves of garlic sliced
2 cups of dry white wine	4 cups of water
2 Tbs of wine vinegar	Juice of 1 lemon

Rub the lamb with half of olive oil, season it with salt and pepper and rub the thyme over the surface of the lamb. Let the lamb sit for an hour to absorb the flavors. Put the white wine, water, vinegar and lemon juice into a pan and bring to the boil. Allow to cool.

Make some slits in the leg of lamb and put some slices of garlic into them, baste with ½ of the liquid, and then rub the lamb with the rest of the olive oil.

Place the lamb between the racks and tie using the 4 S-Hooks. Place disposable pans in bottom of La Caja China to collect juices. Place lamb inside the box, and connect a wired thermometer probe on the leg, be careful not to touch the bone. Cover box with the ash pan and charcoal grid.

Add 16 lbs. of charcoal for Model #1 Box or 18lbs. for Model #2 Box and light up. Once lit (20-25 minutes) spread the charcoal evenly over the charcoal grid. Cooking time starts right now.

After 1 hour (1st hour) open the box, baste, flip the Lamb over, baste again. Dump excess ashes, close the box, and add 9 lbs. of charcoal.

After another hour add 9 lbs. of charcoal.

Do not add any more charcoal; continue cooking the meat until you reach the desired temperature reading on the thermometer.

Fresh Lamb: Rare 140, Medium Rare 145, Medium 160

Easter Leg of Lamb

Apart from being a traditional delicacy in the Easter dinner, Easter lamb is also a part of Jewish religious symbolism.

The ancient tradition of the Pasch lamb inspired among the Christians to make use of lamb meat as a popular food for the festival of Easter.

For the sauce:

2 onions, diced	4 ribs celery, chopped
2 carrots, chopped	4 cloves garlic, smashed
2 bay leaves	4 Tbs olive oil
4 Tbs tomato paste	1 ½ C red wine
4 Tbs butter	4 Tbs flour
4 C beef broth	2 tsp red wine vinegar
Salt/Pepper to taste	

Lamb:

2 - 9lb legs of lamb (bone in)	12 cloves garlic
1 C fresh rosemary	1 C olive oil
¼ C lemon juice	2 Tbs anchovy paste
2 Tbs coarse sea salt	3 tsp black pepper
1 tsp red pepper flakes	

Prepare Sauce:

Sauté onion, celery, carrot, garlic and bay leaves in olive oil, over med-high heat until browned (5 min.) Add tomato paste, cook 1 min, deglaze pan with wine. Reduce to a paste.

Whisk in butter and flour until melted, slowly add broth.

Bring to boil, then reduce to a simmer. Cook 2 minutes, until thickened, then strain and discard solids. Stir in vinegar and season with salt & pepper.

For Lamb:

In food processor, combine all remaining ingredients (except lamb) and puree until smooth. Rinse lamb legs and pat dry. Rub each leg with ½ of paste (both sides).

Place the lamb between the racks and tie using the 4 S Hooks.

Place disposable pans in bottom of Caja China to collect juices.

Place lamb inside the box, and connect a wired thermometer probe in the leg, be careful not to touch the bone.

Cover box with the ash pan and charcoal grid.

Add 16 lbs. of charcoal for Model #1 Box or 18lbs. for Model #2, or Semi-Pro Box and light up.

Once lit (20-25 minutes) spread the charcoal evenly over the charcoal grid. Cooking time starts right now.

After 1 hour (1st hour) open the box, baste, flip the Lamb over, baste again. Dump excess ashes, close the box, and add 9 lbs. of charcoal.

After another hour add 9 lbs. of charcoal.

Do not add any more charcoal; continue cooking the meat until you reach the desired temperature reading on the thermometer.

Fresh Lamb: Rare 140, Medium Rare 145, Medium 160

DO NOT OPEN THE BOX UNTIL YOU REACH THE DESIRED TEMPERATURE

Moroccan Whole Roast Lamb

Recipe by Dee Elhabbassi

Abdellah and Dee Elhabbassi are the owners and Executive Chefs of my very favorite restaurants, Dar Essalam *(translated House of Tranquility) in Wilsonville, Oregon*

The Elhabbassi's moved from Denver to Abdellah's home town of Rabat, Morocco solely to study the finest Moroccan restaurants and traditional recipes before returning to open their own establishment.

The allure of Dar Essalam, besides the outstanding menu, is the genuine hospitality, the obvious passion that the Elhabbassi family has for their work, and the love they feel for their customers. Dee shared this recipe with me as we sat chatting after an amazing dinner at the restaurant. In fact, she insisted that I take her treasured family cookbook home with me to study…with all the little hand-written notes still in it! (How cool is that?)

1 - Grass-fed, three-month-old lamb around 36-40 pounds, skinned. As much surface fat removed as possible.

4 sweet onions, pureed	2 C fresh garlic, ground
2 C butter	2 C olive oil
Salt to taste	3 bunches cilantro, diced
¼ C cumin	½ C coriander
½ C paprika	2 Tbs fresh black pepper

Combine all chermoula ingredients and mix together over medium heat until it forms a paste. (*Chermoula is a Moroccan marinade.*)

Allow chermoula to set overnight.

Rub this mixture over the surface of the lamb making sure to get it evenly distributed, inside and out. Plan on allowing the chermoula to sit on the meat for 48 hours before you cook.

Place the lamb between the racks, tie using the 4 S-Hooks, and place inside the box, ribs side up. Connect the wired thermometer probe on the leg, be careful not to touch the bone.

Cover box with the ash pan and charcoal grid.

Add 16 lbs. of charcoal for Model #1 Box or 18lbs. for Model #2 Box and light up.

Once lit (20-25 minutes) spread the charcoal evenly over the charcoal grid. Cooking time starts right now. After 1 hour (1st hour) open the box flip the Lamb over (ribs down) close the box and add 9 lbs. of charcoal.

After 1 hour (2nd hour) add 9 lbs. of charcoal.

Do not add any more charcoal; continue cooking the meat until you reach the desired temperature reading on the thermometer.

IMPORTANT: Do not open the box until you reach the desired temperature.

Cooking a whole lamb is as much an event, as it is a meal.

With a little planning and preparation, it's no more complicated than cooking a whole pig. Call ahead to your local butcher (if possible, one that specializes in Greek or Middle Eastern meats,) to order your lamb.

Plan on about 4 pounds of raw weight for each guest.

Carving a whole lamb can be intimidating, so take it in sections. You'll need a large area to work with and several serving dishes or big pans.

Cut away the hind legs, then the forelegs. From here you can start carving up the individual sections.

The meat will be very tender, so slicing should not be a problem.

Fresh Lamb: Rare 140, Medium Rare 145, Medium 160

For more amazing Moroccan recipes from the Elhabbassi's kitchen, make sure to visit their website (www.daressalam.org) and pick up a copy of their cookbook, Dar Essalam.

Whole Roasted Goat with Citrus Butter

Recipe by Arthur Jackson

Arthur Jackson is a professional chef based in Chicago, Illinois. He writes for the blog www.thepleasanthouse.com.

This recipe calls for a whole young goat approximately 45 pounds in size. This will easily feed 40 or more guests. Goat meat from this size of animal is extremely tender

There are three simple steps to roasting a whole goat. The first step is to procure and marinate the goat. The second step is to roast the goat the next day. The third step involves brushing the goat with a flavorful citrus butter.

One 45-pound young goat (cabra), cleaned and butterflied

Marinade
½ C chopped fresh rosemary
1 Tbs sea salt
½ C extra virgin olive oil
¼ C chopped fresh garlic
Freshly black pepper to taste

Citrus basting butter
1 whole orange
1 whole lime
½ Lb butter
Freshly black pepper to taste
1 whole lemon
3 cloves garlic, crushed
1 Tbs sea salt

Have your butcher remove the head and shanks of the goat and butterfly the whole animal for you.

Prepare the marinade in a small bowl. Rub the marinade all over the goat, inside and out. Place the goat in a cooler for 24 hours or at least overnight (drain the water, and add ice as needed.)

The day you plan to roast the goat, remove the goat from the cooler and let it come to room temperature before roasting. <u>This is important for even cooking.</u>

Prepare the citrus basting butter by zesting and juicing the orange, lemon, and lime. Add the garlic, zest and juice (minus seeds) to ½ pound butter (two sticks), sea salt, and freshly cracked black pepper in a small saucepan. Gently melt the butter and remove from heat. The citrus basting butter can be kept warm above the coals of La Caja China.

Place goat between the racks and tie using the four S-hooks. Cover box with the ash pan and charcoal grid.

Add 16 pounds of charcoal for a Model #1 Box or 18 pounds for a Model #2 or Semi-Pro Box. Light the charcoal. Once the charcoal is lit (allow 20–25 minutes), spread the charcoal evenly over the charcoal grid.

Cooking time starts right now! (Write down your start time; this will help you keep track of the following steps in the roasting process.)

After one hour add 10 pounds more charcoal (again, write down the time you do this).

Continue to add 9 pounds more charcoal every hour until the internal temperature of the meat reaches 160 F on a meat thermometer for slightly pink meat or 170-180 F for well done (allow 2.5–3 hours).

Lift the charcoal grid, shake it well to remove the ashes, and place it on top of the long handles. Remove the ash pan from the box and dispose of the ashes.

> *Make sure you water down the ashes on the ground, as the hot ashes can cause a fire.*

Brush goat with citrus. Flip the goat over, and baste the skin side of the goat with more citrus butter, and replace the cover to crisp the skin.

Flipping the goat is easily done using La Caja China's patented Rack System. Just grab the end of the rack lift and slide as you pull upward; using the other hand, grab the top end of the other rack and slide it down.

Once again, cover the ash pan with the charcoal grid; do not add more charcoal at this time.

After 30 minutes, lift the lid slightly to see if the skin is browning nicely. You will continue to do this every 10 minutes until the skin is crispy or to your liking.

Once the goat is to your liking, set the lid back on La Caja China at an angle, so the goat stays warm but is not cooking. Let the goat rest for 30–60 minutes (it will still be too hot to touch with bare hands).

Carve the goat and brush with additional citrus butter; season with sea salt.

Hunter's Bear Roast

Friends and family know that I'll cook up just about anything that I can haul home in the back of my truck. So, when things like bear roasts show up on the menu, they're usually not surprised. What does often surprise them is how delicious these wild meats can be, when cooked correctly.

Bears have been hunted since prehistoric times for their meat and fur. In the Middle Ages, the eating of bear meat was considered more a symbolic than culinary act. The paws and thigh of the bear were considered the best parts.

The best bear meat is taken in the spring, and, as bear fat can quickly turn rancid, even when frozen, make sure you trim as much fat as possible from your roast, before cooking.

4 - 4 lb. spring bear roasts	½ C smoked paprika
8 cans beef broth	8 Tbs Au Jus powder
4 tsp pepper	4 tsp seasoned salt
4 sweet onions, minced	

If you don't like the "gaminess" of wild meat (I do) butterfly your bear roasts, place each in an oversized resealable bag with 4 cups of 2% milk and 2 Tbs salt, and refrigerate 24 hours, turning every few hours.

Dispose of milk, rinse the meat, tie the roasts back into their original shape, and proceed with the recipe…

Combine paprika, au jus powder, pepper and salt and rub all sides of bear meat. Wrap each roast in plastic wrap and refrigerate 24 hours.

Allow roasts to rest 2 hours at room temperature.

Place roasts on La Caja China bottom rack, and place disposable drip pans underneath. Tent each roast loosely in foil and place rack in La Caja China.

Insert temperature probe into thickest part of center roast, cover box with the ash pan and charcoal grid.

Add 16 lbs. of charcoal for Model #1 Box or 18lbs. for Model #2, or Semi-Pro Box and light up.

Once lit (20-25 minutes) spread the charcoal evenly over the charcoal grid.

Cooking time starts right now.

Roast to internal temperature of 180 degrees F, adding 10 lbs. of charcoal every hour as required. Remove foil and brown roast 15-20 minutes.

IMPORTANT: Do not open the box until you reach the desired temperature.

Place roasts in disposable roasting pans with one onion each, and pour beef broth over all. Cover pans with foil and return to La Caja China. Add 10 lbs. of charcoal and roast 1 hour.

Remove roasts and allow to rest 20 minutes, then slice against the grain and serve.

Serves up to 24

You can make a great "bear gravy" by combining pan dripping with another package of beef au jus, a small amount of flour, and seasoned salt. Simmer until thickened and serve over boiled root veggies.

ON THE GRILL

Sweet & Spicy Pork Kabobs - 64

Soy-Honey Flank Steak - 65

Brisket Mini-Pizzas - 66

Teriyaki Tri-tip Sliders - 67

Thai Beef Satays - 68

Sizzlin' Buffalo Wings - 69

"Da Best" Burgers - 70

Fritas (*Cuban Burgers*) - 71

Perry's Perfect Steaks - 72

Salmon Fillets with Mustard Glaze - 73

Grilled Oysters - 74

Soft-shell Crabs - 75

Mojo Shrimp Skewers - 76

Sweet Lobster Tails - 77

Sturgeon Kabobs - 78

Grilled Zucchini Boats - 79

Big Island Pork Kabobs - 80

Asian Pork Sliders - 81

Peanut Chicken Satays - 82

Sweet & Savory Bacon Wrapped Dates - 84

Pepper Bacon Bombs - 85

Guacamole-Lime Grilled Chicken - 86

Quick Grilled Flatbread - 87

"The only time to eat diet food is while you're waiting for the steak to cook."

- Julia Child

Multi-Zone Fires

Single Zone

Spread the coals in an even layer across the charcoal grid.

This is the best method to use when roasting meats inside La Caja China, as it provides an even heat to the interior of the box.

For grilling, you would use a single-zone fire for steaks, chicken breasts, or any food that requires a short, hot cooking time. Only used a single-zone fire if all of the meat will finish and be served at the same time.

Even when grilling the types of meat mentioned above, I still like to keep a small "cool zone" at one end of the grill so I can move meat away from flare-ups, melt cheese onto my burgers, etc.

Two-Zone

A two-zone fire is created when your lit coals are spread over one-half to two-thirds of the grilling area.

This is ideal for most types of grilling, especially those foods that need to be seared on the outside, and cooked more slowly on the inside (steaks, spatchcocked chickens, pork tenderloins, ect.)

As mentioned, one benefit of a two-zone fire, when cooking for a crowd, is that you have a "warming area" for foods that are done, or nearly done, to stay warm while another batch is cooking.

If you're grilling at the same time you have meat cooking inside La Caja China, I suggest creating the cool zone in the center of the charcoal grid, with the majority of the burning coals to the right and left.

This allows a more even cooking temperature within the box.

A two-zone fire is preferable, over a three-zone, for the smaller surface area of La Cajita China (Box #3)

Three-Zone

Your best heat control is achieved with a three zone fire, consisting of a hot zone, medium zone, and cool zone.

On the charcoal grid, rake half the coals into a double layer over one third of the fire box, and the rest into a single layer in the center. Leave the remaining third of the grid without coals.

Use the hot zone for searing, the medium zone for finishing, and the cool zone for keeping food warm until serving.

Sweet & Spicy Pork Kabobs

2lbs boneless pork, 1-inch cubes
1 Tbs Worcestershire sauce
2 tsp black pepper
¾ C cider vinegar
4 Tbs lemon juice
2 cloves garlic, minced

¾ C olive oil
1 tsp dried thyme
½ tsp cayenne
¼ C sugar
1 Tbs oregano
1 tsp salt

Mix together all ingredients, place in sealable bag and refrigerate 24 hours; thread onto skewers.

Grill over hot coals, basting with reserved marinade, for 4-5 minutes; turn and grill another 4-5 minutes.

Makes 6 servings

Soy-Honey Flank Steak

½ C red wine vinegar
¼ C minced fresh ginger
1 Tbs salad oil
4 cloves garlic, pressed
Lime wedges (optional)

¼ C soy sauce
3 Tbs honey
1 tsp black pepper
2 lbs flank steak

In a gallon-size zip-lock, mix together vinegar, soy sauce, ginger, honey, oil, garlic, and pepper. Add steak (close bag) and turn to coat.

Refrigerate 6-8 hours, turning several times. Let stand at room temperature, turning occasionally, for 30 minutes.

Drain steak; discard marinade. Lightly oil La Caja China grill, and lay on meat above a solid bed of hot coals (you can hold your hand at grill level only 1 to 2 seconds.)

Cook meat, turning to brown evenly, until pink in the thickest part for med-rare (125°F), 5 - 6 minutes per side.

Transfer steak to a cutting board and garnish with lime wedges. Thinly slice meat across the grain to serve. Offer lime wedges to squeeze over individual portions to taste.

| Rare - 120°F | Medium Rare - 125°F | Medium - 130°F |

Brisket Mini-Pizzas

Leftover barbecue makes for tasty pizza toppings, and prepared pizza dough helps make this a quick and easy crowd pleaser!

Grill these appetizers once your first layer of coals are white, and before adding fresh charcoal, to keep the crowds satisfied while the main dish is cooking to perfection in La Caja China.

Alternatively, you can make two family-size pizza instead of sixteen individual ones.

½ C extra virgin olive oil	4 clove garlic, minced
2 pkg "ready bake" pizza dough	4 C shredded provolone
2 C shredded pecorino romano	2 C Texas Brisket Sauce
4 C leftover brisket, finely chopped	

In bowl, combine oil and garlic. Cut dough into eights. On lightly floured surface, roll each piece into 4-inch circle.

Brush with oil mixture.

Place grills on La Caja China, and spread coals to both ends, leaving a 1/3 area in the middle with just a thin layer of coals.

This is your "cooking area."

Place dough, oiled side down, on grill and cook until golden, about 5 minutes. Flip dough and brush each with 1 Tbs sauce, spread 1/4 cup provolone cheese over the grilled side, and top with 1/4 cup brisket; sprinkle with pecorino Romano cheese.

Cover and cook until bottoms are golden and crisp, and cheese is melted, about 5 minutes.

A disposable steamer pan makes a great "cover" for the recipe. Two will cover an entire third of the rack area.

Makes 16 "mini" or 2 whole pizzas.

Teriyaki Tri-tip Sliders

Teriyaki is a cooking technique used in Japanese cuisine in which foods are broiled or grilled in a sweet soy sauce marinade (tare in Japanese). The tare is traditionally made by mixing and heating soy sauce, sake or mirin, and sugar or honey.

The sauce is boiled and reduced to the desired thickness, then used to marinate meat, which is then grilled or broiled.

4 beef tri-tips (2 lb/ea.)	2 tsp dry mustard
4 C soy sauce	1 C brown sugar
3 C thinly sliced onion	2 C sake
2 C mirin	4 Tbs minced garlic
4 Tbs thinly sliced fresh ginger	2 tsp pepper

Pour in soy sauce, sugar, onion, sake, mirin, garlic, ginger, pepper, and mustard into 4 a gallon-size resealable bags. Add one tri-tip to each bag, and seal.

Chill 24 hours, turning occasionally.

Lay tri-tips on a lightly oiled La Caja China grill over a solid bed of coals, turning every 5 minutes, until 125° to 130° on an instant read thermometer, or about 25 minutes.

Transfer tri-tip to a cutting board. Let rest about 5 minutes, and then cut across the grain into thin, slanting slices.

Place 1-2 slices on a split potato roll, top with *Simple Tangy Coleslaw*, or pickled ginger, and serve.

32 Servings

Thai Beef Satays

Satay (SA-tay), a very popular shish kebab style dish that has long been popular in Indonesia and Thailand. It is most frequently associated with Thai food, where satay made from cubes of beef, chicken, or lamb may be dipped in a traditional peanut relish or sauce.

Satays are grilled or barbecued over a wood or charcoal fire, then served with various spicy seasonings, like our Spicy Thai Peanut Sauce,

2 lb sirloin tips	60 bamboo skewers
2 Tbs red curry Paste	26 oz coconut milk
2 Tbs fish sauce	2 Tbs minced ginger

Cut sirloin into thin strips

In a medium saucepan, heat coconut milk with the curry paste. Stir until smooth and bubbling. Turn off heat. Add fish sauce and minced ginger.

Stir well and pour into shallow dish. Add the beef, making sure each piece is well coated.

Cover and refrigerate for six hours or overnight.

Soak bamboo skewers in cold water 2 hours before grilling to keep them from burning on grill.

Thread meat onto skewers and grill on La Caja China for 3 minutes on each side or until done.

Serve 2 skewers per guest.

Sizzlin' Buffalo Wings

This is the original spicy Buffalo chicken wings recipe from the Anchor Bar, in Buffalo NY, where they first appeared in October, 1964. The recipe has been modified slightly for the grill.

36 chicken wings, separated	1 Tbs vegetable oil
1 tsp salt	1 C all-purpose flour
1 ½ Tbs white vinegar	¼ tsp cayenne pepper
¼ tsp garlic powder	1 tsp Tabasco sauce
¼ tsp Worcestershire sauce	¼ tsp seasoned salt
6 Tbs Frank's Red Hot Sauce	6 Tbs unsalted butter
celery sticks	blue cheese dressing

Mix all the ingredients for the sauce in a pan, bring to a simmer, stirring, and then cool.

Toss the wings with the oil, and salt. Place into a large plastic bag, add the flour, and shake to coat evenly. Remove from the bag, shaking off excess flour.

Place wings on hot grill, turning several times until golden brown.

Remove wings from grill and place them in a sealed bowl with the sauce and shake well. S

Serve immediately with blue cheese and chilled celery sticks.

"Da Best" Burgers

Fletcher Davis of Athens, Texas, is believed to have sold hamburgers at his café in the late 1880s, then brought them to the 1904 St. Louis World's Fair. The McDonald's hamburger chain claims the inventor was an unknown food vendor at that same World's Fair.

The hamburger bun was invented in 1916 by a fry cook named Walter Anderson, who later co-founded White Castle in 1921.

3 Tbs lemon pepper	1 Tbs ground thyme
1 Tbs paprika	1 tsp granular garlic
½ tsp sugar	½ tsp seasoned salt
½ tsp fresh black pepper	pinch cayenne pepper
1lb ground beef, 20% fat	

Mix spices, except for salt, with ground beef about an hour before cooking, to allow flavors to marry.

Form ½ inch thick patties, slightly larger than the buns, and sprinkle with salt just before grilling.

Sear your patties on each side over a high heat until a crust forms. This should take about one to one-and-a-half minutes.

Move patties to a cooler part of the grill and cook another ten minutes, flipping once.

Fritas

Recipe by Roberto Guerra

These Cuban burgers are great to cook on the top grill while you roast the pig inside the box. The chorizo really makes it special.

4 lb ground beef	2lb Cuban chorizo
2 lb ground pork	¾ C milk
¾ C bread crumbs	1 tsp paprika
3 Tbs minced onion	2 eggs
4 tsp salt	1 tsp Worcester sauce
½ tsp black pepper	

Combine ground meats and chorizo.

Soak bread crumbs in milk, beat eggs and add to the milk together with all the remaining ingredients.

Add to the meat mixture and mix well using the hands. Shape into medium hamburgers.

Place them in the fridge for a couple of hours.

Serve on medium size rolls topped with julienne potatoes.

There is a big difference between Cuban chorizo and Mexican chorizo. Mexican chorizo has a grainier texture and tends to fall apart when you split the casing where as Cuban chorizo has more of a solid sausage texture. Also, Cuban chorizo has no hot peppers, and is packed with lots of fresh cilantro.

Perry's Perfect Steaks

To grill the perfect steak, you get what you pay for. Go with t-bone, rib-eye or NY strips. If you can find a butcher that ages their beef 30 days, you'll taste the difference.

3lbs NY Strip Steaks, 2" thick.   Coarse sea salt
Fresh ground black pepper

Remove steaks from refrigerator 1 hour before cooking, pat dry and allow to rest at room temp. Oil La Caja China grill and heat to highest temp. If you can hold your have six inches above the grill and count to two, it's not hot enough! Add some oak and/or pecan chips, ¼ cup of each, on the coals 5 minutes before steaks.

Butter:

½ stick of sweet cream butter   1 Tbs lemon juice
¼ cup chopped Italian parsley   2 Tbs minced garlic
1 Tbs Worcestershire sauce   dash red pepper flakes

Melt butter, stirring to combine ingredients, and pour into a baking pan.

Cooking: place steaks on grill and cook until lightly charred (about two minutes) do not move steaks until the first side is finished cooking, use tongs to turn. Flip steaks to second side and grill 2 more minutes.

Remove from grill and place in baking pan, dredging both side in the butter. Return steaks to grill, sprinkle each side with sea salt and pepper, and finish cooking looking for an internal temp of 115d.

Once steaks reach that (2-3 addition minutes per side) move them back to the baking pan, dredge in butter again, and allow to rest 10-15 minutes at room temp.

To serve, drizzle a little of the butter and juice mixture (from the pan) onto your cutting board and slice steaks thinly across the grain. Pour a little of the butter/juice onto a plate, top with a fan of steak slices, and spoon a bit more butter over the top.

Sprinkle with remaining chopped parsley and serve immediately.

Salmon with Mustard Glaze

Native American Indian tribes of the Pacific Northwest coast and the Columbia River relied on salmon as major food source for thousands of years.

Salmon was a foundation for life, culture, economy, and spirituality.

1 Tbs olive oil	2 C chicken broth
4 salmon fillets, 3/4" thick	2 Tbs Dijon mustard
4 Tbs balsamic vinegar	¼ C brown sugar

In pan, combine broth, vinegar, mustard and brown sugar. Heat to a boil. Cook over medium heat 10 min. or until mixture is slightly thickened and reduced to 1 cup.

Start 5lbs of coals on La Caja China, allow coals to turn white. Spread coals into a "Two Zone" fire.

Grill salmon on a well oiled grill, skin side-up on "hot" side of La Caja China, cooking until browned, about 3 min.

Turn over and season with coarsely ground pepper and brush with ½ of glaze.

Cook 2 minutes, then move to "cool" end of grill and cook two more minutes, still skin down.

Spoon any remaining glaze over salmon, and serve.

Grilled Oysters

For generations before the pioneer settlers arrived, Chinook Indians gathered oysters around what it now Willapa Bay and camped in the area that is now Oysterville, Washington. Oysters were typically set in the hot coals of the fire until the shell popped open, then the oyster meat would be removed with a knife or pointed stick. Similarly, oysters can be cooked in their shells on your Caja China's grill racks. The heat from the grill steams the oysters and pops the shells open, while poaching the oyster inside.

They make a great appetizer while your salmon or brisket is cooking inside the box!

4 dozen oysters, scrubbed	Cocktail sauce
1 C butter	1 Tsp seasoned salt
1 tsp lemon pepper	Lemon wedges

Melt butter with seasoned salt and lemon pepper

Place your La Caja China grill racks, oiled, over the hot coals (don't do this just after adding coals, but wait until coals are evenly white.)

Place oysters, unshelled, on grill. Oysters have a "cup" side (like a bowl) and a "lid" side (flat), the cup side should be down so as not to lose all the yummy juices.

Get your condiments close to the grill on another table and make sure everyone has put on their gloves. Have aluminum pie pans available, if you like, to use as plates. When shells open (in about 3 minutes), use an oyster knife to detach oyster from top shell, and discard.

Then encourage everybody to dig in, topping oysters with their favorite condiments, or seasoned butter. Continue cooking the oysters in batches until they're gone. Oysters that don't open should be discarded.

If you're having trouble getting your oysters to "sit up straight" on the grill, you can fashion some small rings out of aluminum foil to place each oyster in, while it's cooking.

Soft Shell Crabs

As crabs grow, their shells cannot expand, so they molt the exteriors and have a soft covering for a few of days when they are vulnerable and considered usable as soft-shells. Fishermen often put crabs beginning to molt aside, until the molting process is complete, in order to send them to market as soft-shells. A New England staple, the sweet and subtle briny flavor of fresh soft-shell crab is truly the essence of the sea.

24 jumbo soft-shell crabs	4 tsp salt
4 tsp black pepper	1 ½ C butter
4 tsp hot sauce	4 Tbs lemon juice

With a pair of kitchen shears, remove the eye sockets and the lower mouth. Carefully lift up the apron and remove the gills. Gently rinse with cool water and pat them dry.

Sprinkle the crabs with the salt and pepper.

Melt butter with hot sauce and lemon juice and stir to mix. Remove from the heat and cool for several minutes.

Put the crabs in a bowl and pour the butter sauce over them. Let stand for about 20 minutes.

Place crabs on La Caja China grill over a medium-hot fire. Cover and cook for four minutes.

Turn the crabs over, cover and cook for about four to five minutes or until the crabs are slightly crusty.

Baste with the butter sauce and serve.

Serves 24

Mojo Shrimp Skewers

One warning about roasting a whole pig, brisket, or just about anything in La Caja China....for the last forty-five minutes of cook time, there's an ever-expanding cloud of mouth-watering aroma outside the box. This will gather friends, family, and neighbors you've never met, in seagull-like crowds to your yard.

The best way to deal with these culinary paparazzi, is to toss the grill racks over the coals and prepare a few simple, tasty appetizers.

One of my favorites is bacon-wrapped mojo shrimp, inspired by La Caja China's special Adobo Criollo spice blend. Simple to prepare, you can assemble dozens of these skewered treats between the time you fire up the roaster, and the time the aroma of yummy goodness begins wafting through your neighborhood.

2 lbs sliced bacon	64 raw prawns, tail off
2 C Traditional Cuban Mojo	¼ C Adobo Criollo
32 skewers, soaked	

Rinse raw prawns and drain. In a large bowl, toss prawns and Adobo Criollo spices.

Wrap each prawn in ½ slice of bacon, and thread two wraps into each skewer, touching, and with skewer through both the bacon and the shrimp.

Once coals on La Caja China have turned completely white, but before adding unlit charcoal, lay skewers in grill, with only the meat over the coals.

Grill 3-5 minutes, until bacon is cooked, flip, and cook 2-3 more minutes.

Watch carefully to make sure that neither the bacon, or the skewers (if wood) are burning.

Remove from grill and let rest on a paper-towel covered platters 2-3 minutes before serving.

You can find metal "double skewers" at most stores that have a BBQ section. These look like giant tuning forks, and are ideal for this type of grilling.

Sweet Grilled Lobster Tails

A surf-n-turf dinner with grilled fresh lobster tails and filet mignon is a surefire hit.

This grilled lobster is perfect for any occasion. If you don't have a lot of experience grilling shellfish, then this easy recipe is for you.

Lobster tails only take a few minutes to grill, so wait until your steaks, or other entree are done cooking before grilling lobster tails.

12 lobster tails	½ C olive oil
¼ C fresh lemon juice	½ C butter
1 Tbs crushed garlic	1 tsp sugar
1/2 tsp salt	½ tsp black pepper

Combine lemon juice, butter, garlic, salt, and pepper over med-low heat and mix until well blended, keep warm.

Create a "cool zone" with minimal coals at one end of La Caja China, brush meat side of tails with olive oil, place onto grill and cook for 5-7 minutes, depending on the size of the lobster tail. Make sure to turn once during cooking process.

After turning, baste meat with garlic butter 2-3 times.

The shell should be bright red when they are finished. Remove the tails from the grill, and using large kitchen shears, cut the top part of the shell open.

Serve with warm garlic butter for dipping.

Sturgeon Kabobs

Sometimes referred to as "poor man's lobster" because of its sweet, succulent meat, the massive sturgeon is a prehistoric survivor of the ice age, and the largest freshwater fish in the world. Ancient Romans believed sturgeon to be an aphrodisiac with life-extending properties.

While I can't make any promises about your love life, I guarantee that these kabobs will be the hit of your next barbecue!

4 lbs raw sturgeon	4 lbs sliced bacon
12 metal double-skewers	2 bottles Teriyaki sauce
4 cans pineapple chunks	

Cut sturgeon into 1-inch cubes. Wrap a half slice of bacon around it, and skewer, making sure to pin the bacon, as well as the meat, (so the bacon won't fall off.)

Take one piece of pineapple and skewer, then another bacon wrapped sturgeon, repeat until skewers are full.

Place filled skewers in a baking dish and pour the teriyaki sauce over them, turning to coat well, and let sit for 1 hour.

Place skewers on La Caja China grill, over white coals, and baste with sauce while cooking.

Cook 8-10, turning and re-basting once. Do not allow the bacon to burn.

If you're using wooden skewers, make sure you soak them for about 20 minutes before grilling.

Grilled Zucchini Boats

Summer squash has its ancestry in the Americas. However, the varieties of squash typically called "zucchini" were developed in Italy, many generations after their introduction from the "New World."

The first records of zucchini in the United States date to the early 1920s. It was almost certainly brought over by Italian immigrants and probably was first cultivated in the United States in California.

2 medium zucchini	1 slice of bread, cubed
¼ C bacon, crumbled	3 Tbs diced green chilies
¼ C minced onion	¼ C chopped tomato
6 Tbs Italian cheese blend	4 Tbs grated asiago
1 pinch dried basil	Seasoned salt to taste
Black pepper to taste	

Prepare the grill for indirect heat. Start 5lbs of coals on La Caja China.

When coals are white, spread into a "Two Zone" fire, leaving a coal-free cooking area in the middle. While coals are heating, place the zucchini in a pot with enough water to cover. Bring to a boil, and cook 5 minutes. Drain, cool, and cut in half lengthwise. Scoop out the pulp to about 1/4 inch from the skin. Chop pulp.

In a bowl, mix the zucchini pulp, bread pieces, bacon, jalapeno, green chile peppers, onion, tomato, and Italian cheese. Season with basil, seasoned salt, and pepper. Stuff the zucchini halves with the pulp mixture. Seal each stuffed half in aluminum foil.

Place foil packets on the prepared grill over indirect heat (center.) Cook 15 to 20 minutes, until tender.

Remove from foil and place over direct heat 1-2 minutes to score with grill marks. Sprinkle with asiago cheese and serve.

For a great main dish, add 1 cup of cooked, crumbled, sweet Italian sausage to step 3. Rinse cooked sausage in hot water to reduce grease.

Big Island Pork Kabobs

1 lb Pork tenderloin
1 clove garlic – minced
2 lbs whole mushrooms
2 tsp lime juice
1 Tbs minced parsley

1 C margarita mix
1 lg red bell pepper
2 Tbs butter - softened
1/8 teaspoon sugar

Combine margarita mix, coriander, and garlic.

Cut pork into 1-inch cubes, place in a heavy plastic bag, and pour marinade over to cover. Marinate overnight.

Blend together well the butter, lime juice, Splenda, and parsley; set aside.

Thread pork cubes onto skewers, alternating with mushrooms and pepper, cut into eighths.

Grill over hot coals, basting with butter mixture, for 10-15 minutes, turning frequently.

If you're using bamboo skewers, soak them in water 20-30 minutes before using.

Asian Pork Sliders

Sliders (mini burgers) are one of my favorite barbecue appetizers. Quick, simple, and given to nearly unlimited variations, our guests can assemble their own favorite toppings from a pre-arranged "burger buffet" and all I have to do is flip the meat and serve.

The intense heat from La Caja China is perfect for quick-cooking crispy outsides, while allowing the interior meat to stay moist.

2 lbs ground pork	1 C diced green onion
2 tsp garlic powder	2 Tbs soy sauce
2 tsp brown sugar	1 tsp cornstarch

Mix all ingredients (except soy sauce) and form 16 equal patties. Brush each patty with soy sauce, and grill over white-ash-covered coals, turning once.

Serve with hoisin sauce and cucumber spears.

To take this recipe up a notch, add 2 Tbs of sesame oil to my Simple Tangy Coleslaw (see recipe) and include a couple of tablespoons on each slider.

I like to chill the seasoned meat and then spread it on an oiled cutting board, using a rolling pin for an even 1/4 inch thickness.

Then, I just grab a biscuit cutter, and voila...perfectly round sliders!

Peanut Chicken Satays

Satays are and Asian-inspired street food that pack a lot of flavor onto a small stick. Traditionally a grilled skewer with pieces of seasoned meat, seafood or even tofu, the satay is the "New York Hotdog" of the Pacific Rim.

The bite-size chunks make satays easy to eat, and they work just as well as an appetizer as they do a main course.

4 Tbs olive oil
2 tsp ginger powder
2 Tbs curry powder
20 wooden skewers, soaked
2 lbs chicken thighs, cut into strips

4 Tbs sesame oil
2 tsp powdered garlic
Butter lettuce leaves
Fresh cilantro leaves

Peanut sauce:

2 C chunky peanut butter
¼ C brown sugar
1/3 C limes juice

½ C soy sauce
¼ C sweet chili paste
2/3 C hot water

Combine oils, ginger, garlic, and curry powder in a shallow mixing bowl, stir to combine.

Place the chicken strips in the marinade and gently toss until well coated.

Cover and let the chicken marinate in the refrigerator overnight.

Thread the chicken pieces onto the soaked skewers working the skewer in and out of the meat, down the middle of the piece, so that it stays in place during grilling.

Brush La Caja China grill with oil to prevent the meat from sticking.

Grill the satays for 3 to 5 minutes on each side, until nicely seared and cooked through.

Serve on a platter lined with lettuce leaves and cilantro; accompanied by a small bowl of peanut sauce on the side.

For the sauce:

Combine the peanut butter, soy sauce, chili paste, brown sugar, and lime juice in a food processor or blender.

Puree to combine, and drizzle in the hot water to thin out the sauce.

Pour the sauce into individual serving bowls.

If serving as a main dish, add a side of steamed jasmine rice, and fresh veggies.

Sweet & Savory Bacon Wrapped Dates

Everything tastes better with bacon, and dates are no exception! Be warned, we serve these as appetizers while the pig or lamb is roasting, and they go fast!

1 lb thick-sliced bacon, cut in half	1 lb pitted dates
4 ounces gorgonzola cheese	32 toothpicks

Slice dates up one side, and open them up. Pinch off a piece of cheese, and place it into the center of the date.

Close the halves of the dates, and wrap a half-slice of bacon around the outside, secure with a toothpick.

Lay a single sheet of foil over La Caja China grill grates, and add the wraps in a single layer.

Grill until bacon starts to crisp, then flip each wrap over.

When the second side is crisped, remove to a platter lined with paper towels, allow to cool slightly, and then get the heck outta the way, 'cause folks will trample you to get them!

Pepper Bacon Bombs

These bite-sized bombs are always a hit. Roasting take a bit (but not all) of the fire out of the peppers, and leaves a sweet, smoky, spicy treat that will have your guests begging for more.

20 fresh jalapenos
8oz. Cream Cheese
1/8 Sweet Onion (diced)

20 Cheddar Lit'l Smokies
2 Lbs. Bacon (½ strip ea)
1 Tbs. Sugar

Soften cream cheese and blend in sugar and onions.

Slice Jalapenos in half, lengthwise, and spoon 1 teaspoon of cream cheese mixture into each side.

Place 1 smokie between the two halves, and press closed.

Wrap in bacon, securing each with a toothpick.

Lay a single sheet of foil over La Caja China grill grates, and add the bombs in a single layer.

Grill until bacon starts to crisp, then flip each bomb over.

When the second side is crisped, remove to a platter lined with paper towels.

Allow to cool slightly, and serve.

If these "bombs" have a little too much heat for you, use a half a pepper for each. Grill the "open" side first and turn quickly before all the gooey goodness melts out.

Guacamole-Lime Grilled Chicken

Recipe by Stephanie Arsenault

Stephanie is a freelance food and travel writer based out of Western Canada, and writes one of my very favorite food blogs, SEARED (http://seared.ca/) This is a blog for foodies, by foodies & about foodies!

If you can't get enough of the Food Network, trying new recipes, or playing with your pepper grinder, you should probably subscribe to this blog. Stephanie loves to bring her readers only the tastiest and coolest grub and gadgets.

3 ripe avocados	2 limes
10 cherry tomatoes	1-2 jalapenos, minced
1 clove garlic, finely minced	½ small red onion, diced
4 boneless, skinless chicken breasts	1 Tbs olive oil
¼ tsp salt	¼ tsp cayenne
Lime slices and fresh cilantro (optional)	

Halve tomatoes, then each half cut into quarters.

Cut each avocado in half and remove each pit. With a spoon, scoop the avocado flesh into a medium sized bowl.

Squeeze the juice from one of the limes into the bowl, and with two butter knives or a pastry cutter, mash the mixture until the avocado is smooth with some small chunks. Stir in the tomatoes, jalapenos, garlic, onion, and some salt, to taste. Cover and place in the refrigerator until ready to use.

Build a 2-zone fire on La Caja China. In a small bowl, mix juice of the other lime, olive oil, salt, and cayenne. Brush the mixture on both sides of the chicken breasts and place on the grill.

Cook for about five minutes, flip, and cook for another five minutes, until golden and cooked through.

Remove chicken from grill, place on serving plates, and top with guacamole. Garnish with lime slices and fresh cilantro.

Quick Grilled Flatbread

As far as recipes go, it doesn't get much easier than this. Grilled flat bread makes a great addition to brisket, pulled pork, satays, or just about any roasted meat!

2 cans prepared biscuit dough   2 Tbs olive oil
Coarse sea salt

Separate the biscuits and roll out each piece to 1/8 inch thick round.

Lightly brush one side of each round with olive oil and place the rounds oiled side down on La Caja China grill.

Grill the flatbread for 1-2 minutes, until lightly browned, brush the side that's facing up with olive oil and flip.

Grill for 1-2 more minutes, brush top with oil, remove from the grill and sprinkle the hot bread with salt before serving.

SIDE DISHES

"Nothing would be more tiresome than eating and drinking if God had not made them a pleasure as well as a necessity."

- Voltaire

Bubba's Best Baked Beans

According to tradition, sailors brought "cassoulet" from the south of France, or the regional bean stew recipes from northern France and the Channel Islands.

Bean hole cooking as practiced in Maine's logging camps used stone-lined fire pits where the bean pots would be buried to cook overnight or longer.

32oz canned navy beans	½ lb salt pork, cubed
1 can diced tomatoes	3 strips bacon
1 can diced green chilies	2 Tbs chili paste
½ cup brown sugar	1 tsp dry mustard
1 Tbs garlic	2 tsp hot sauce

Soak salt pork 4 hours, rinsing and replacing water often.

In a large pot, sauté bacon and pork (diced) until lightly browned.

Add garlic, sauté 1 to 2 minutes longer.

Add tomatoes, chili paste, sugar, mustard, & hot sauce.

Add beans and bring to a simmer.

Cool and refrigerate 24-48 hours.

Warm & serve.

FRIJOLES NEGROS

(black beans)

2 lbs. black beans	2 bay leaves
20 C of water	8 tsp. salt
1 green pepper	1 tsp. pepper
1 C olive oil	1 tsp. oregano
1 large onion	4 Tbs. vinegar
8 garlic cloves	4 Tbs. olive oil
4 Tbs sugar	1 C red wine

Wash the beans and soak in water. When the beans swell, cook in the same water until soft. (45 minutes.)

Heat the oil in a frying pan, add onion, chop up or mash garlic and chop up green pepper.

Add 1 cup of the beans to the pan and mash. Add this to the beans together with the salt, pepper, oregano, bay leaves and sugar.

Allow to boil for a 1 hour then add the wine and vinegar allowing to cook uncovered for a while.

Add 4 tbs. of olive oil just before serving.

Serves approximately 20

Sautéed Butter-Rum Plantains

Plantains are a staple food in the tropical regions of the world, treated in much the same way as potatoes and with a similar neutral flavor and texture.

2 C dark rum
Salt
1/4 cup canola oil

1 C dark brown sugar
2 Tbs butter, diced
6 very ripe plantains

Peel and slice plantains on the bias, 1/2-inch thick. Plantains should be very ripe (almost black.)

In a heavy skillet, melt the butter over medium heat. Add half of the plantains and fry them in a single layer for about 4 minutes on each side.

Remove with a slotted spoon and keep warm in a bowl. Repeat.

Drain and wipe oil from the same pan, combine the rum, brown sugar, butter, and salt. Stir over medium heat until the sugar has dissolved, then bring the mixture to a vigorous boil.

Cook for 2 minutes, until slightly thickened.

Return the plantains to the pan and stir to coat them evenly with the sauce.

Allow to cool slightly, and serve.

Plan on one plantain per serving

ARROZ BLANCO

(white rice)

Rice is a staple food on the Latin Caribbean islands. For a simple dish that won't overshadow the rest of the menu, plain white rice is hard to beat and easy to make.

Cuban rice is made rich by cooking rice with garlic-infused olive oil.

3 lb. rice	6 cloves garlic
9 C water	9 Tbs oil
3 Tbs salt	

Heat oil in a shallow casserole and brown garlic. Take it off the heat and remove garlic from the oil.

Add water and salt to the oil and bring to a rolling boil.

Add the washed rice and stir.

Bring to a rolling boil again, cover and cook over low heat for approximately 30 minutes.

Serves 20

Vickie's Favorite Brisket Beans

This is a great "next day" recipe after serving smoked brisket. My BBQ partner Chris saves the burnt ends from his briskets specifically for this recipe. Make sure you save the broth from the brisket pans as well. Chill it overnight and skim off the excess fat before adding to this recipe.

1-lb smoked brisket, cubed
1 C chopped onion
1 C brown sugar bbq sauce
2 Tbs yellow mustard
16oz kidney beans, drained
16oz butter beans, drained
16oz diced tomatoes, drained

10 slices bacon, diced
1 C brown sugar
¼ C hot sauce
1 tsp chili powder
1 tsp black pepper
28oz baked beans
2 cups brisket broth

Sautee onions & bacon, add brisket cubes to warm.

Add all remaining ingredients (except beans), simmer 30 minutes.

Add beans, mix gently, and transfer into a heavy baking dish.

Bake at 350 for 1 hour, uncovered.

I typically brew up my own sauce, but in case of emergencies - my preferred bottled brands for this recipe are Sweet Baby Rays Brown Sugar BBQ, *and* Frank's Red Hot Sauce.

Pop Fairrington's Hor-De-Voors

Okay, these don't have anything to do with La Caja China or barbecue, but they're so dang good, I just had to add them.

Pop Fairrington made them up at elk camp one year, and I've been addicted ever since!

    5oz smoked salmon, diced
    8 oz pineapple cream cheese
    2 ½ whole avocados,
    20 Ritz crackers

Dice the salmon. Pit and mash avocados coarsely with salt, pepper and garlic.

Take a cracker, spread with cream cheese, place a chunk of salmon on one half, and a chunk of avocado on the other.

Try to stop eating them…good luck.

Pineapple cream cheese can be tricky to find, but you can make your own with a small can of crushed pineapple, a little sugar, and 8oz of cream cheese.

Make sure that you press as much liquid as possible out of the pineapple, or your cream cheese will end up runny.

Smothered Sweet Corn

2 C sugar
1 large onion, chopped
1 medium bell pepper, chopped
1 gallon whole kernel corn, drained
2 stick butter, salted

In a large pot (preferably cast iron), melt the butter.

Add the sugar and cook over medium heat until the mixture starts to turn a light brown.

Add onion and bell pepper, and sauté for 5 minutes.

Add the corn. Stir often to prevent it from sticking to the bottom.

Cook until the mixture becomes a golden brown.

This may take up to 45 minutes.

Simple Tangy Coleslaw

The term "coleslaw" arose in the 20th century as a partial translation from the Dutch term "koolsla", a shortening of "koolsalade", which means "cabbage salad"

Coleslaw is generally eaten as a side dish with foods such as barbecue, French fries, and fried chicken. It is also a common barbecue sandwich ingredient.

    1lb shredded green cabbage
    ¾ C mayonnaise
    ¼ C rice wine vinegar
    5 tsp sugar
    1 tsp toasted sesame seeds

Heat vinegar and sugar until sugar is dissolved, allow to cool.

Add mayonnaise, blend well, and chill again.

Toss with cabbage, sprinkle with toasted sesame seeds, and serve immediately.

If you want to get all "foodie" and impress your guests at your next brisket bbq… add ½ cup crumbled blue-cheese to this recipe. It's a knockout with the beef!

Cebollas Curtidas

(pickled onions)

Cebollas curtidas (pickled onions) is a simple, yet elegant way of preparing onions for the perfect combination of sweet and sour to complement any savory or spicy meal.

4 large red onions, peeled and halved
2 C fresh lime juice
Salt

Thinly slice the onions and place into a heat-proof, non-reactive bowl.

Pour boiling water over them, wait 10 seconds, then pour the onions into a large strainer.

Return the drained onions to the bowl, pour on the lime juice and stir in the 1 ½ teaspoons salt.

Cover and place in the refrigerator until serving time.

Before serving, taste and season with additional salt if you think necessary.

Makes 7 cups

Hawaiian Rice

From the mid 1860's when the whaling industry's domination of Hawaii's economy ended, until the 1920's, rice was second in value and acreage only to sugar cane in the Hawaiian Islands.

The islands of Kauai and Oahu proved most suitable to rice cultivation, because of their abundance of water.

2 ½ C jasmine rice	5 C chicken stock
1 ½ C diced pineapple	2 C diced ham
6 Tbs. butter	Salt & pepper
½ C slivered almonds	

Cook rice in chicken stock until stock is absorbed.

Brown pineapple and ham in butter.

Stir in rice and season, to taste, with salt and pepper.

Add almonds, stir well and bake for 15 minutes in a 350 degree oven.

Serves 8-10

Fresh Corn on the Cob

Really, what needs to be said? It's awesome.

    4 ears fresh corn, shucked
    1 Tbs sweet butter
    Salt to taste

Wrap one ear of corn in tinfoil, smear with butter and salt lightly.

Toss inside La Caja China for the last 30 minutes of meat cooking time.

Tostones de Platano Verde
(fried green plantains)

The tradition of the tostone came to Cuba from African slaves. In the Congo, the people prepare plantains in the exact same way, even to this day.

4 plantains	2 cups peanut oil
1 tsp salt	4 Tbs garlic mojo

Peel the plantains and cut into 1inch pieces.

Fry at 365F for 5 minutes, or until they begin to brown.

Drain plantains on paper towel.

Flatten them using a tostonera or the bottom of a metal can and fry again at 385 for approximately 3 minutes.

Drain again and sprinkle with salt and garlic mojo.

For softer fried plantains, soak for a few minutes in salted water after the first fry, drain and fry again.

A tostonera *is a wooden (or sometimes plastic) press used to make flatten plantain sections into tostones.*

Whole Hog Dirty Rice

This recipe is one of the reasons I love roasting whole pigs in La Caja China.

The broth is simply amazing, with a richness that is impossible to get with any smaller cut of pork.

1 lb roasted pig, chopped	2 stalks celery, minced
1 Can cream of mushroom soup	1 C raw Jasmine rice
2 "Cans" reserved pork broth	1 sweet onion, minced

Combine raw rice, veggies, and soup in a heavy pan. Use the empty soup can to add broth.

Cook covered at medium approximately 90 minutes, or until rice is cooked.

Stir once or twice while cooking

Add roasted pork during last 5 minutes of cooking.

Serves 4-6

Ma Geisert's Cheesy Potatoes
Recipe by Shar Geisert

As the one who hung the nickname "Bubba" on me, I owed it to my good friend Shar "Ma" Geisert to include this fabulous dish. She served this one holiday dinner...and owned me from that point on.

A quick and simple recipe with amazing results!

1 stick butter	1 can cream of chicken soup
1 C cheddar cheese, shredded	¼ C chopped sweet onion
1 ¾ C sour cream	2lbs frozen cubed hashbrowns
Salt & pepper	

Preheat oven to 350d

Melt the butter, mixing in all of the ingredients except the hashbrowns.

Once combined, add hashbrowns.

Spray a 13x9 pan, add all this stuff, and bake 1 hour, 15 min or until potatoes are brown and crunchy on the edges.

A handful of cooked, diced bacon, or some freshly roasted red bell paper can be added for a nice twist.

Savory Watermelon Salad
Recipe by Terry Ramsey

Our BBQ partner-in-crime, Terry Ramsey, grills this refreshing treat as a side dish or dessert. It's always a hit!

5 lbs seedless watermelon
Extra-virgin olive oil
2 C fresh arugula, washed
1 C goat cheese, crumbled
¼ cup chopped green onion

¼ C balsamic vinegar
Coarse sea salt
Fine black pepper
2 Tbs white sugar

Slice watermelon into 1-inch thick cubes.

Pour the vinegar into a small saucepan with sugar and bring to a simmer over medium-high heat.

Cook until reduced to a thick syrup consistency. Set aside.

On the "cool end" of a 2-zone fire, grill watermelon about 2 minutes per side, until grill marks appear.

Transfer to a plate and season with salt.

Combine all ingredients onto salad plates and finish each salad with a very light drizzle of olive oil and balsamic syrup, and chopping onions.

Dust with black pepper and serve immediately.

Quick Saffron Rice

Saffron rice is a favorite side dish to roast chicken in Thailand. This quick (and fat free) recipe uses a bit of turmeric to balance the much more expensive saffron.

2 C Thai jasmine rice	3 ½ C chicken stock
½ tsp salt	½ tsp turmeric
½ tsp saffron threads	1 clove garlic, minced

Pour stock into a medium-size lidded pot, and heat on high.

While stock is coming to a boil, add the turmeric, saffron, and garlic. Stir well. Add the rice and stir.

Return to a boil, then reduce heat to low and cover tightly with a lid.

Cook 12-15 minutes, or until the rice has absorbed the liquid, then turn off the heat and place lid on tight.

Allow to sit 5-10 minutes, or until you're ready to eat. The residual heat inside the pot will finish steaming the rice, and the rice will stay warm in this way for an hour or more.

Before serving, remove the lid, fluff rice with a fork, and taste-test before adding salt.

To check for doneness, insert a butter knife straight down into the pot and push the rice aside.

If you see liquid, it still needs more time to cook.

Grilled Pineapple Salsa

Okay, when most folks think of salsa, they're thinking tomatoes, tomatillos, ect.
This sweet, fresh-fruit alternative is a refreshing change of pace, and goes quite nicely with the pork tenderloin recipes in this collection.
It's also wonderful over a grilled, sliced chicken breast.

1 large pineapple	1 red bell pepper
1 med jalapeño (optional)	1 small red onion, diced
½ C chopped cilantro	2 small limes, juiced
Sea salt	

Skin pineapple, core, and cut into 1-inch rounds

Place the pineapple slices, bell pepper, and jalapeño on La Caja China grill, at the "cool" end of a 2-zone fire.

Cook the pineapple until lightly browned on both sides, about 2 to 4 minutes per side.

Remove from the grill, chop medium, and place in a medium sized bowl. Cook the peppers until completely charred all over. Remove from the grill to a paper or Ziploc bag and seal.

When the peppers are cool enough to handle, about 5 minutes, remove their skins and chop the red pepper medium and the jalapeño finely.

Add to the bowl with the pineapple.

Add the onion, cilantro, and lime juice to bowl and toss until well combined.

Season with salt and serve.

Sweet Roasted Apples

A simple, delicious treat, apples have been roasted for as long as there's been fire and apples.

This is a very traditional recipe, which tends to always include raisins and spices, along with some form of traditional sweetener such as sugar or a honey.

I like my roasted apples sweet, so I added both.

6 lg. Braeburn apples	3 Tbs chopped dates
3 Tbs walnuts, chopped	3 Tbs brown sugar
1/4 C. honey	1 Tbs lemon juice

Wash and core apples. Mix walnuts and raisins, place 1 spoonful in each apple.

Mix honey and lemon juice; pour 1 spoonful in each apple. Drizzle apples with a little water.

Wrap each apple in foil, and place around whole pig, or pork shoulder in La Caja China for the last 90 minutes of cooking time.

Remove, unwrap, and serve 1/2 apple with each serving of pork.

Most any apple can be used for roasting. My mom always used big green apples, but I've found that Braeburns tend to hold their shape, texture, and color the best, when slow roasted.

Bubba's Easy Guacamole

Guacamole is an avocado-based dip which originated in Mexico. It is traditionally made by mashing ripe avocados with a molcajete (mortar and pestle) with lime juice and salt.

Guacamole was made by the Aztecs as early as the 1500s. After the arrival of the Spanish conquistadors, guacamole became popular in Spain.

When I say "easy" it really doesn't get much easier than this. In this grill guy's opinion, the avocado is one ingredient where less really is better than more.

You can add salsa, peppers, or whatever to your guacamole, but for me, it's all about the avocado!

3 Haas avocados	1 lime, juiced
½ tsp sea salt	½ tsp garlic powder
¼ tsp black pepper	

Halved, seed, peel, and dice avocados.

Mix all ingredients with a fork until coarsely blended, chill briefly, and serve.

Monteria Criolla

Recipe by Roberto Guerra

This is a very popular recipe in Cuba to use up the leftovers of the roast suckling pig.

1 pig's head	4 pig's foot
1 lb roast pork	1 C capers
1 3 onions	1 large green pepper
¼ tsp cumin	3 cloves garlic
1 ½ C of dry wine	1 ½ C tomato sauce
½ C oil	¼ tsp oregano
1 tsp freshly ground pepper (optional)	1 bay leaf

Cut the pig's head and skin into six or eight pieces.

Heat oil and sauté the minced onion and crushed garlic. Add the minced green pepper and the tomato and cook for a few minutes over medium high heat.

Add the remaining ingredients and cook over medium heat for one hour or until the pieces of skin are tender.

Spoon over bowls of Arroz Blanco, and serve immediately.

Congri

Recipe by Roberto Guerra

Also know as Moros Y Cristianos, this is one of the national dish of Cuba, Alluding to the Crusades, Moros (the Moors) refer to the black beans and Cristianos (the Christians) to the white rice.

This dish is a must on Christmas day.

1 ½ lb black beans	10 C rice
1 lb bacon	12 C water
1 green pepper	1 bay leave
4 tsp salt	¼ tsp Oregano
1 tsp cumin	8 cloves garlic
2 medium onions	

Wash beans and soak overnight with half of the green pepper.

Cook beans until tender in the same water. Strain the beans and save three cups of the broth.

In a pan, cook the chopped bacon until crispy. Remove meat and half of the oil, sauté the minced onion, garlic and green pepper in the hot oil until the onion is golden.

In a large pot add the beans, 3 cups of broth, salt and oregano. Place the pot over medium heat until it comes to boil.

Add the rice and stir to prevent from sticking to the bottom of the pot.

Cover and cook over medium heat until rice is tender.

Just before serving, add the crispy bacon and oil to the congri,

Stir again and let it cool five minutes before serving

Meathead's Buttermilk Cornbread

Recipe by Guy "Dr. Biggles" Prince

Outdoor cooking and photography enthusiast Guy Prince has been playing with fire, food, and cameras since he could walk. He's been blogging as "Dr. Biggles" on one of my favorite food sites, MeatHenge (www.meathenge.com), for over seven years.

A published writer and food photographer, Pitmaster Guy has been featured in major newspapers, magazines, and books...and he loves every minute of it!

When I have a question on barbecue, grilling, or cast-iron cooking, I go to MeatHenge and ask Dr. Biggles!

2 C buttermilk	1 egg
¼ C bacon fat	1 Tbs mayonnaise
2 C yellow corn meal	3/4 tsp baking soda
Pinch of Kosher salt	

Preheat oven to 450, lower oven rack to bottom.

Combine dry with dry and wet with wet. Allow buttermilk and egg to come to room temp.

Rub a 10" or 12" cast iron skillet with liberal amounts of bacon fat. Mix your wet ingredients with dry to form batter, and pour into room temperature skillet.

Bake, uncovered, 25 minutes or so, until done.

Let rest a while and slice.

Serve with a pat of butter over top with honey *slooping* down and puddling on the plate.

Life has never been so good!

If you don't have a cast iron skillet, you cannot reproduce this cornbread. Stop now and either give up, or find one. Ask Mom or Gramma if you need to! – Guy

SAUCES, RUBS & MOPS

"If more of us valued food and cheer and song above hoarded gold, it would be a merrier world."
— J. R. R. Tolkien

North Carolina Barbecue Sauce

In the Carolinas, the barbeque meat is pork, and the barbeque sauces are matters of hot debate even from one town to the next.

Some sauces are thin and vinegary, while some regions add ketchup, or even mustard.

This is the recipe I grew up with.

- 1 qt cider vinegar
- 12 oz ketchup
- 2/3 C packed brown sugar
- 2 Tbs salt
- 1 tsp each: black pepper, dry mustard
- ¼ C lemon juice
- 1 Tbs red pepper flakes
- 1 Tbs smoked paprika
- 1 Tbs onion powder

Bring all ingredients to the boil, and then simmer for 30-45 minutes, stirring frequently.

Allow to cool, and serve or bottle.

Okay, if you promise not to tell my customers, I'll let you in on a little secret...

When I run out of my homemade bbq sauce, and my Caja and I are running late to an important date, there are a couple of "off the shelf" sauces that I'm willing to pair with my favorite recipes...

Sweet Baby Rays (brown sugar), or Stubbs Mesquite.

Memphis-Style Barbecue Sauce

Memphis barbecue sauce has its own distinctive flavor, as well. Though the specific ingredients will vary from cook to cook, Memphis sauce is usually made with tomatoes, vinegar, and any countless combination of spices.

Memphis sauce is poured over pulled pork, or served along side of dry ribs.

1 Tbs butter
¼ C finely chopped onion
1 ½ C ketchup
¼ C chili sauce
4 Tbs brown sugar
4 Tbs molasses
2 Tbs yellow mustard
1 Tbs fresh lemon juice
1 Tbs Worcestershire sauce
1 Tbs liquid hickory smoke
½ tsp garlic powder
½ tsp salt
½ tsp ground black pepper
1 tsp chili powder
dash cayenne pepper

Bring all ingredients to the boil, and then simmer for 30-45 minutes, stirring frequently.

Allow to cool, and serve or bottle.

Texas Brisket Sauce

Texas is famous for tender slow-smoked brisket. Sauces are usually thin, spicy, and mixed with intensely flavorful pan drippings.

½ C brisket drippings (defatted)
½ C vinegar
1 Tbs Worcestershire sauce
½ C ketchup
½ tsp hot pepper sauce (Franks)
1 lg onion, diced
2 cloves of garlic, pressed
1 Tbs salt
½ tsp chili powder
Juice of one lemon

Combine all ingredients.

Simmer, stirring occasionally, for 15 minutes.

Allow to cool and refrigerate 24-48 hours before using.

Sweet Hawaiian Pork Sauce

Kalua Pork (or pig) is one of my favorite Hawaiian dishes.

It's a smoky, salty pulled pork dish served over white rice, with a variety of optional sauces - from a simple liquid smoke and water wash, to elaborate sauces that highlight the tropical fruits and sugar cane of the islands.

> 15oz peaches & juice
> 15oz pineapple & juice
> 16oz peach preserves
> 1 cup brown sugar
> 2 Tbs liquid smoke
> 2 Tbs minced garlic
> 1 Tbs red pepper flakes

Combine all and bring to boil.

Lower heat and simmer on low until sauce has begun to thicken.

Keep warm until serving. Drizzle over pulled pork.

For a very classy presentation, shred the pork, top with whole pineapple rings, baste well with sauce, sprinkle generously with crushed macadamia nuts, and return to La Caja China 5-10 minutes to brown the top.

Spicy Thai Peanut Sauce

This easy no-cook peanut sauce has a terrific authentic Thai taste. It is spicy and peanutty, and is perfect as a dipping sauce for chicken, shrimp, and beef.

3 C creamy peanut butter
3/4 C coconut milk
1/3 C fresh lime juice
1/3 C soy sauce
1 Tbs fish sauce
1 Tbs hot sauce
1 Tbs minced fresh ginger root
5 cloves garlic. minced

In a bowl, mix the peanut butter, coconut milk, lime juice, soy sauce, fish sauce, hot sauce, ginger, and garlic.

Simmer 10 minutes, and serve.

Garlic Mojo

Mojo (pronounced mo-ho) is the Spanish name for a number of Latin sauces made with vinegar or citrus juice and garlic.

It is a traditional accompaniment to the starchy root vegetables of the Hispanic Caribbean, as well as a marinade for pork, chicken, and other local meats.

    8 garlic cloves
    1 tsp salt
    1/4 C sweet orange juice
    1/8 C of fresh lime or lemon juice.

Chop up the garlic very thinly or crush using a mortar and pestle or food processor with salt to form a thick paste.

In a mixing bowl, combine the garlic paste and juice, and let the mixture sit at room temperature for 30 minutes or longer.

Garlic Blue Cheese Sauce

¾ C heavy cream
1 medium garlic clove, thinly sliced
6 oz blue cheese, crumbled
Freshly ground black pepper

In a medium-sized saucepan over medium-high heat, bring cream and garlic just to a boil.

Lower heat and simmer until the cream coats the back of a spoon, approximately 5 to 10 minutes.

Remove from heat.

Stir in the crumbled blue cheese. Season to taste with the pepper.

Serve Garlic Blue Cheese Sauce on the side of any beef dish.

Makes approximately 2 cups.

> *Note: This can be made two days in advance. Cover and refrigerate. Bring to room temperature before serving.*

Sour Cream Horseradish Sauce

Horseradish, a relative of mustard, wasabi, broccoli, and cabbages, is thought to be native to southeastern Europe and western Asia, but is popular around the world.

Horseradish has been cultivated since antiquity both for its medicinal properties, and as a condiment on meats in Germany, Scandinavia, and Britain.

The name is derived from the old method of processing the root called "hoofing." Horses were used to stamp the root tender before grating it.

½ C prepared horseradish (or to your taste)
1 Pt (2 cups) sour cream
2 Tbs fresh squeezed lemon juice
1 tsp salt

In a medium-sized bowl, combine horseradish, sour cream, lemon juice, and salt; thoroughly mix.

Refrigerate until ready to serve.

Gorgonzola Dipping Sauce

Blue cheese is believed to have been discovered by accident. The caves in which early cheeses were aged shared the properties of being temperature and moisture controlled environments.

Gorgonzola, a favorite of mine, is one of the oldest known blue cheeses, having been created around 879 AD

1 C crumbled blue cheese
2/3 C sour cream
½ C mayonnaise
1 clove garlic, minced
1 oz white wine
2 tsp Worcestershire sauce
1 tsp salt
1 tsp fresh ground black pepper

In a glass or plastic bowl, combine all ingredients, using the salt and pepper to finalize the taste and the white wine to set the consistency.

What is a Rub?

In the food of the Southern United States, dry rub is often used on grilled or barbequed meats.

Dry rubbed ribs are a popular dish, but steaks, burgers or pork chops are also given flavor through a spice rub.

Most typical Southern style spice rubs include chili and cayenne pepper, garlic and onion powder, salt and black pepper, paprika and dry mustard.

Although the quantities of hot ingredients can be adjusted, rubs are often an extremely spicy mix that add a powerful kick to meat.

La Habana Pork Rub

The habanero chili pepper most likely originated in the Yucatán Peninsula and its coastal regions.

The chili's name is derived from the name of the Cuban city of La Habana, which is known as Havana in English.

The habanero's heat, its fruity, citrus-like flavor, and its floral aroma have made it a popular ingredient in hot sauces and spicy foods.

5 Tbs coarse sea salt
5 Tbs dark brown sugar
3 Tbs sweet paprika
3 Tbs coarse black pepper
2 Tbs ground cumin
2 Tbs dried oregano
1 fresh diced habanero chili pepper

Combine all, mix well, and rub entire batch onto 4-6lb pork shoulder.

Habanero peppers can cause a painful reaction to some folk's skin, and never, ever get any juice on your face or eyes.

I recommend wearing plastic gloves when preparing these, and other extremely hot peppers, and immediately wash the prep area and any utensils that you used.

Perry's "Burnin' Love" Rub

"Burnin' Love BBQ" is the name of the catering business that my fellow pit-masters, Chris Renner, Terry Ramsey, and I operate. Really, it's just an excuse to stand around in smoke and cook a lot of pigs and briskets…but don't tell our wives, okay?

This is our secret pork shoulder rub. Apply is generously to the inside of a butterflied shoulder, roll it, tie it, and apply more rub to the outside. You MUST allow the rubbed shoulder to rest in the fridge at least overnight so that the rub will help form that wonderful "bark" while roasting.

Finally, after it's done cooking and you've pulled, chopped, or shredded the meat, give it one last sprinkle for an intense, spicy flavor.

   ¼ C coarse sea salt
   ¼ C light brown sugar
   2 Tbs garlic powder
   2 Tbs onion powder
   2 Tbs Italian seasonings (spicy, if you can find them)
   4 Tbs smoked paprika
   2 Tbs coarse black pepper
   1 Tbs hickory salt
   1 tsp cayenne powder

Mix well.

Good for 6-8lbs of pork.

Renner's Amazing Brisket Rub

Christopher Renner is the unquestionable brisket king of our team, and possibly anywhere else on the planet, as well. His rub recipe is as simple as it is wonderful...

For 4 full briskets (7-8lbs each):

1 C fine sea salt
1 C coarse pepper
1 C granulated garlic
1/4 C smoked paprika
1/4 C cayenne

Smoke brisket(s) with a mix of oak and pecan.

Chris says that the difference between good brisket and amazing brisket is patience.

Double wrap the finishing brisket in foil, wrap that in a towel, and let the whole thing rest in a closed cooler for 1-2 hours.

Then, once you've unwrapped it, allow it to sit and cool slightly for 15-20 minutes for slicing or pulling.

Smokey Beef Rib Rub

2 Tbs brown sugar
2 Tbs black pepper
2 Tbs smoked paprika
2 Tbs chili powder
2 tsp onion salt
2 tsp garlic powder
2 tsp celery salt
2 tsp seasoning salt

Mix well and rub both sides of ribs, wrap tightly in plastic wrap, and refrigerate overnight.

Bring ribs to room temperature before cooking.

Hellfire Cajun Rub

Dry rubs can be applied to meat, fish, or poultry or added to pasta, jambalaya, or any dish that you want to spice up.

This rub makes a great seasoning for fried, baked, or grilled chicken, as well.

8 Tbs smoked paprika
4 Tbs cayenne powder
4 Tbs dried parsley
4 Tbs black pepper
2 Tbs garlic powder
6 Tbs fine sea salt
2 Tbs ground cumin
4 Tbs dried oregano
1 tsp ghost chili powder (to taste)

Combine all the ingredients, mix well and store 24-48 hours, in an airtight container, before using.

Wear gloves, and use extreme caution, when handling ghost chili powder, even breathing the tiniest amount will be painful.

This chili has been measured at over 1 million Scoville units (by comparison, Jalapeno peppers are about 4500 Scoville units.)

This is the hottest Chili Powder available anywhere.

Start with just a teaspoon...trust me.

A Word about Mops

Barbecue "Mops" or basting sauces, are vinegar (or other) based liquids that are applied to meats during the slow cooking process of traditional barbecue, to keep the meat moist and add flavor.

Legend has it that President Johnson liked his barbecue, and often called upon his favorite Pitmaster to cook for hundreds of guests.

The meal would be cooked on a forty square-foot open air fire pit. The cook would cover every inch of this in ribs, briskets, halved pigs, and just about any other meat he could think of.

To keep all that meat moist he mopped it with a thinned sauce...using a real mop. Hence the barbecue term, "mop."

Today you can buy a miniature tool that looks like a kitchen mop to mop your meat. the cotton fibers hold the thin mop sauce and make it easy to dash large amounts on at once.

If you ask the barbecue experts, they'll tell you that rubs and mop sauces are key to every Championship BBQ team.

Carolina Basting Mop

Mopping (basting) the meat while cooking helps keep it moist and adds additional flavors. Never use a basting brush on any meat that has a dry rub applied, as it will brush off seasonings.

Mop the meat every 30 minutes for the first half of the cooking time.

2 qts water
2 qts apple cider vinegar
2 qts vegetable oil
1 C liquid smoke
½ C salt
¼ C cayenne pepper
¼ C black pepper

Combine all ingredients and bring to a simmer. Allow to cool overnight, and warm before using.

Use as a rib/chicken baste, or sprinkle on pulled or chopped barbecued pork before serving.

Basic Vinegar Mop

2 C cider vinegar
½ C vegetable oil
5 tsp salt
4 tsp red pepper flakes

Combine all ingredients and bring to a simmer, allow to cool overnight to help the flavors marry.

Keep warm and apply to meat before you close La Caja China, when you flip the meat, and again when the meat is done cooking.

Allow the meat to rest at least 30 minutes to soak up the mop.

Perry's Pig Pickin' Mop

This recipe is for the whole hog, but in reality, it can be used for all types of pork.

If you're preparing smaller cuts of pork, simply scale back the quantities. Use as a marinade, and injection, a mop, and finally, as a wash on the finished meat, just before serving.

1 qt. apple juice
1 qt. apple cider vinegar
¼ C fine sea salt
¼ C garlic powder
¼ C smoked paprika
1 C light oil
½ C mesquite liquid smoke (unless you have smoker)
1 tsp black pepper
1 tsp cayenne pepper

Simmer for 15-20 minutes.

Keep warm and apply to pig before you close La Caja China, when you flip the pig, and again when the pig is done cooking.

For a more traditional "Eastern" North Carolina mop, use only the apple juice, vinegar, salt, and cayenne. For South Carolina, add 1 cup prepared mustard to that.

Beef Rib Mop

3/4 C brown sugar
1/2 C bottled barbecue sauce
1/2 C ketchup
1/2 C cider vinegar
1/2 C Worcestershire sauce
1 C water
1 Tbs salt
1 Tbs chili powder -- optional
1 Tbs paprika

Combine all ingredients in a quart jar. Shake to blend thoroughly.

Best if made ahead of time; will keep indefinitely in the refrigerator.

This mop is great for brisket, as well. Keep warm and apply to ribs before you close La Caja China, when you flip the ribs, and again when the ribs are done cooking.

Makes 1 quart

Traditional Cuban Mojo

Recipe by Roberto Guerra

This classic Cuban seasoning sauce makes a flavorful marinade for meats and poultry. Traditionally this is made with sour oranges, cumin, lots of garlic.

With larger cuts (pork shoulder, or whole pig & lamb) it can be injected into the meat 12-24 hours before cooking.

  1 C sour orange juice
  1 Tbs oregano
  1 Tbs bay leaves
  1 garlic bulb
  1 tsp cumin
  3 tsp salt
  4 oz of water

Peel and mash the garlic cloves. Mix all the ingredients and let it sit for a minimum of one hour.

For marinade, add the above recipe to 1 ½ gallons of water, and 13 oz. of table salt.

Blend all ingredients and let it sit for a minimum of one hour, strain and inject, or place meat in a cooler and pour marinade to cover overnight.

You can replace the sour orange juice with the following mix: 6 oz. orange juice, 2 oz. lemon juice.

Hawaiian Mojo

This is my variation of Roberto's Cuban Mojo. "Real" luau pig is typically seasoned with just salt and liquid smoke.

I like the sweet, Polynesian overtones that this marinade/mop adds to the pork.

> 1 C orange juice
> 1 C pineapple juice
> ½ C mesquite liquid smoke
> 1 Tbs oregano
> 1 Tbs minced garlic
> 1 tsp cumin
> 3 tsp salt
> 4 oz. of water

Mix all the ingredients and let it sit for a minimum of one hour.

For marinade/injection, add the above recipe to 1 ½ gallons of water, and 13 oz. of table salt.

Blend all ingredients and let it sit for a minimum of one hour, strain and inject, or place meat in a cooler and pour marinade to cover overnight.

After injecting/soaking the pig or shoulder, apply a salt rub all over the meat, use Kosher salt or coarse sea salt.

Cajun Whole Pig Marinade

Cajuns are an ethnic group mainly living in Louisiana, consisting of the descendants of Acadian exiles. Cajun food is rural, well seasoned, often spicy, and tends to be very hearty.

Whole hog roasting of often the centerpiece of a coup de main (French for "to give a hand") when the community gathers in order to assist one of their members with time-consuming or arduous tasks like a barn raising, harvest, or assistance for the elderly or sick.

With a large Cajun influence in my own family tree, this unique and wonderfully diverse cuisine is close to my own heart.

1 Pint warm water	2 Tbs salt
6 Tbs powdered garlic	6 Tbs powdered onion
3 oz crab boil seasoning	6 oz Worcestershire
6 oz Tabasco sauce	6 Tbs Cajun seasoning
1 lb fresh garlic, peeled	

Mix all ingredients, except peeled garlic. Allow to rest overnight.

Cut garlic cloves in half lengthwise. Moisten and coat the cloves in the marinade. With a slender, sharp knife, cut small slits in the skin and into the meat. Insert a ½ clove garlic in each slit. Insert garlic into all parts of the pig.

Inject marinade into pig every 2-3 inches. Brush interior of pig with ½ of remaining marinade.

Reserve remaining marinade to sprinkle over chopped pork before serving.

Allow the pig to marinade in a cooler 24 hours.

May your coffin be made of the finest wood, from a century-old cypress tree…that I shall plant tomorrow!
- *Cajun Toast*

I

APPENDIX
TABLES & CHARTS

Approximate Servings Per Pound

(Raw weight)

Pork, Shoulder Bone-in	3
Pork, Back Ribs	1.5
Pork, Country Style Ribs	2
Pork, Spareribs	1.5
Pork, Whole	1.5
Beef, Standing Rib	2.5
Beef, Ribs	2.5
Beef, Tri-Tip	4
Chicken, Whole	3
Lamb, Leg (bone in)	1
Turkey, Whole	¾

When planning a meal, it is always better to purchase too much meat than not enough.

Always be prepared for people with larger appetites.

One trick I use is to add a "mystery" guest for every 4 confirmed. In other words, I plan 5 portions for 4 people, 10 portions for 8, 15 for 12, etc.

If there are leftovers, the cooked meat will keep in the refrigerator for several days or the unused portions may be frozen for long term storage.

Wood Smoking Chart

Wood type	Characteristics	Use with
Alder	Very delicate with a hint of sweetness.	Good with fish, pork, poultry, and light-meat game birds. Traditionally used in the Northwest to smoke Salmon.
Apple	Slightly sweet but denser, fruity smoke flavor.	Beef, poultry, game birds, pork (particularly ham).
Cherry	Slightly sweet, fruity smoke flavor.	Good with all meats.
Hickory	Pungent, smoky, bacon-like flavor.	Good for all smoking, especially pork and ribs.
Maple	Mildly smoky, somewhat sweet flavor.	Good with pork, poultry, and small game birds
Mesquite	Strong earthy flavor.	Most meats, especially beef. Most vegetables.
Oak	The second most popular wood to use. Heavy smoke flavor. Red Oak is thought the best by pitmasters.	Good with red meat, pork, fish and heavy game.
Pecan	Similar to hickory, but not as strong.	Good for most needs.
Cherry	The flavor is milder and sweeter than hickory.	Good on most meats.
Black Walnut	Very heavy smoke flavor, usually mixed with lighter wood like pecan or apple.	Good with red meats and game.

RESOURCES

La Caja China Grills & Accessories
http://www.lacajachina.com/

Roberto's Throwdown with Bobby Flay
http://www.lacajachina.com/

Griller's Index
www.grillersindex.com/

Turkey step-by-step
www.cyberbilly.com/meathenge/archives/000538.html

Burnin' Love BBQ – La Caja China Recipes
www.burninlovebbq.wordpress.com

La Caja China Videos
http://youtube.com/lacajachinatv

La Caja China fan page (Facebook)
http://facebook.com/lacajachina87

Twitter
http://twitter.com/lacajachina

Elk Mountain Books Publishing
http://www.elkmountainbooks.com

INDEX

La Caja China Semi-Pro Model

This new model has all the same distinct capabilities as the original La Caja China model #2, but an updated sleek look - diamond-cut metal exterior, steel angle legs with powder coating paint and bolt mounted handles - and some new bells and whistles like the drain valve, that makes it even easier to use.

The following items are included; Top Grill (2), Wind Deflector, HD Charcoal Grid, Reinforced Charcoal Tray, Oversize Rack, Smoke Pistol, Smoker Thermometer, Wood Cartridges Combo, Ash & Charcoal Disposal system, Aluminum Serving tray, Set of hooks and Chain (to clamp meat in the racks).

This unit ships with the ash and charcoal disposal system.

Ships fully assembled

La Caja China Model #1

Up to 70 lbs Pig, 16-18 whole Chickens, 4-6 Turkeys, 8-10 Pork Ribs Slabs, 8-10 Pork Shoulders or any other type of meat or fish.

The Following Items Are Included: Charcoal Pan & Grid, Large Dripping Pan, 2 Stainless Steel Grills, 4 S/S Hooks, one Marinating Syringe, 2 Large Metal Handles & Instructions.

Length: 48" Width: 24" Height: 20" Inside Depth: 8 3/4". Boxes are made of BC Plywood, lined with Marine Aluminum Gauge .032.

Also available in galvanized caribe

La Caja China Model #2

The largest capacity of the La Caja China Models

Up to 100 lbs Pig, 16-18 whole Chickens, 4-6 Turkeys, 8-10 Pork Ribs Slabs, 8-10 Pork Shoulders or any other type of meat or fish.

The Following Items Are Included: Charcoal Pan & Grid, Large Dripping Pan, 2 Stainless Steel Grills, 4 S/S Hooks, one Marinating Syringe, 2 Large Metal Handles & Instructions.

Length: 48" Width: 24" Height: 24" Inside Depth: 12 3/4". Boxes are made of BC Plywood, lined with Marine Aluminum Gauge .032.

La Caja China Model #3

For smaller groups and events

Up to 16 lbs Turkey, 2-3 whole Chickens, 2 Pork Ribs Slabs, 1 -2 Pork Shoulders, or any other type of meat or fish.

The Following Items Are Included: Stainless Steel Pan & Grid, S/S Pan Holder Marinating Syringe & Instructions.

Length: 28" Width: 14 1/2" Height: 29" Inside Depth: 8 3/4". Boxes are made of BC Plywood, lined with Marine Aluminum Gauge .032

Also by Perry P. Perkins

About the Author

Perry P. Perkins comes from a long line of professional chefs. As a third generation gourmand, he focuses his love of cooking on barbeque, traditional southern fare, and fresh Northwest cuisine.

Perry has written for hundreds of magazines, everything from Writer's Digest and Guideposts, to American Hunter and Bassmaster Magazine. His inspirational stories have been included in twelve Chicken Soup anthologies, as well.

His books include the novels *Just Past Oysterville*, and *Shoalwater Voices*, his new humor collection, *Elk Hunters Don't Cry*, and a short story anthology, *Four From Left Field*.

Perry is the Portland Writing Examiner, and you can read more of his work at www.perryperkinsbooks.com.

His books are available at bookstores online.

For more great recipes, and tips for cooking with La Caja China, visit Perry's blog: www.burninloveblog.com, and his menu planning service, www.hautemealz.com

hautemealz.com
THE "AMAZING MEALS MADE EASY" SYSTEM!

Take the hassle out of menu planning, save time and money, and enjoy amazing meals made easy, all for just five bucks a month!

- Weekly 7-meal illustrated menu plan of delicious, nutritious dinners!

- Itemized shopping lists, organized by store section!

- Tips & videos on meal preparation, storage ideas, and shopping!

how it works

Each week we ll email you a 7-menu plan of delicious, nutritious dinners from our *Hautemealz, Haute & Light, SugarSmart, or Personal Plan* menu, along with a beautiful, full-color photo of each dish.

Every menu comes with a complete shopping list, organized by store section, a breakdown of the active and inactive time required to prepare each recipe, and a list of common pantry items you ll need that week

Tips on shopping, storage, and preparation accompany many of the recipes, as well, and even more are posted, as articles, videos, and Q&A, on the hautemealz.com Blog.

Take the hassle out of menu planning, and enjoy amazing meals made easy!

pricing

Programs in the hautemealz.com system are available with menus and shopping lists for 2, 4, or 6 servings, each for a monthly subscription rate of just $5.00. That s right five bucks a month! Want to get both the *hautemealz* and the *haute & light* menu each week?

Still just five bucks a month!

You can subscribe online via PayPal, or with a major credit card. Please contact us for personal check or money order payment options. You may cancel at any time.

Amazing meals made easy!

www.hautemealz.com

30803154R00096

Made in the USA
Lexington, KY
17 March 2014